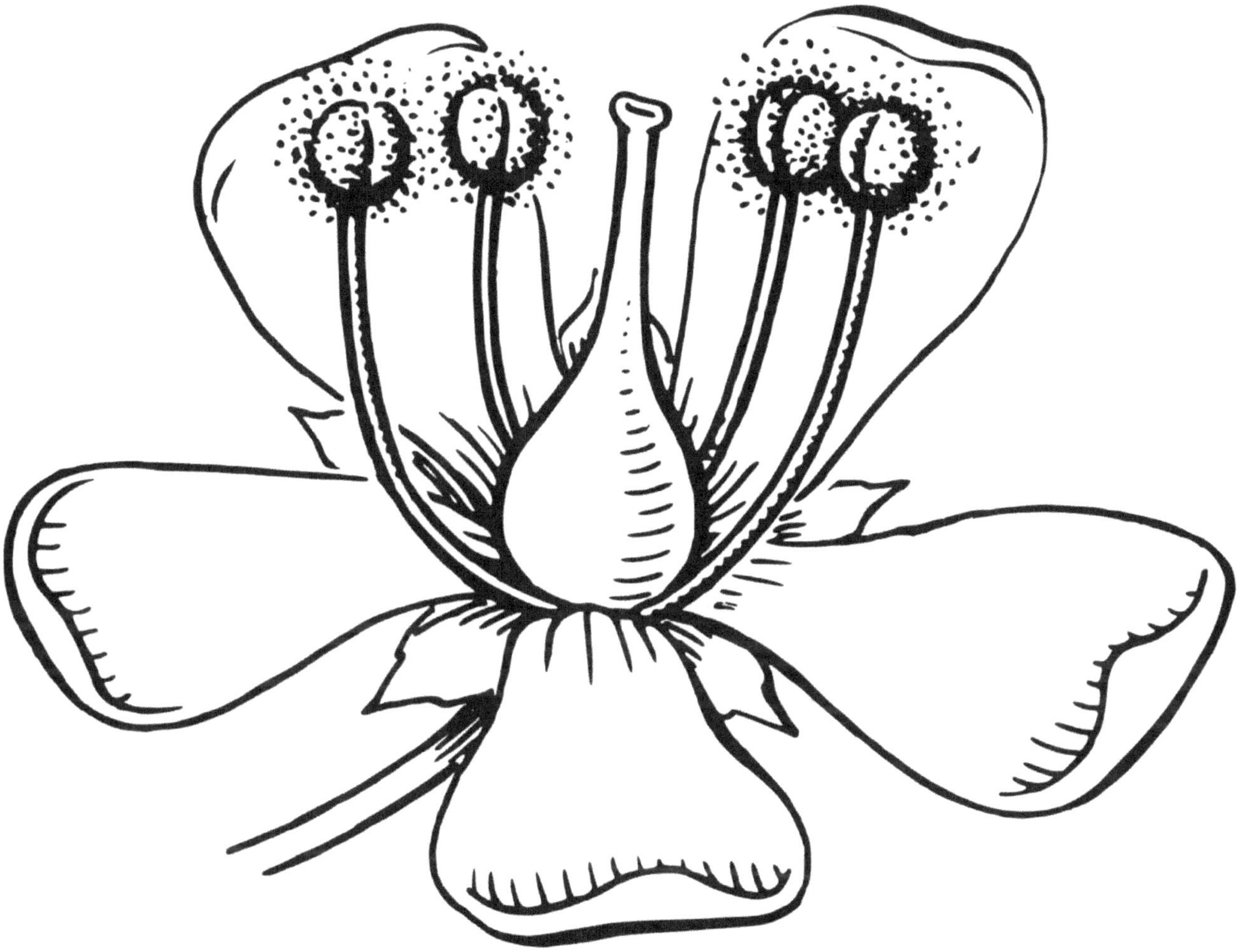

Floral Fantasies

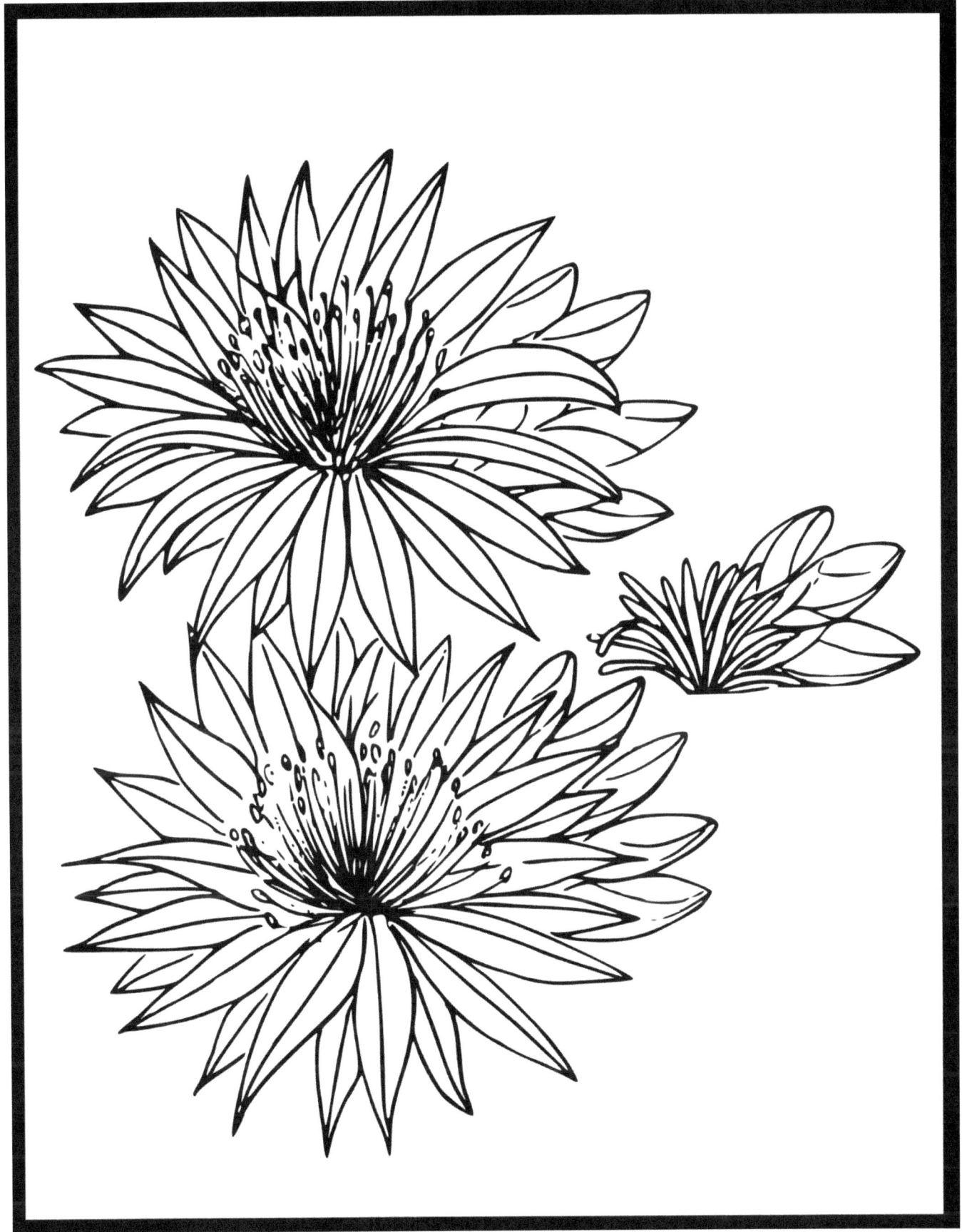

Floral Fantasies

K. H. Burkett

Copyright © 2018 K. H. Burkett

All rights reserved.

ISBN: 1727646819
ISBN-13: 978-1727646818

DEDICATION

This coloring book is dedicated to everyone that loves to color. Without you I wouldn't have a reason to make these books.

Floral Fantasies

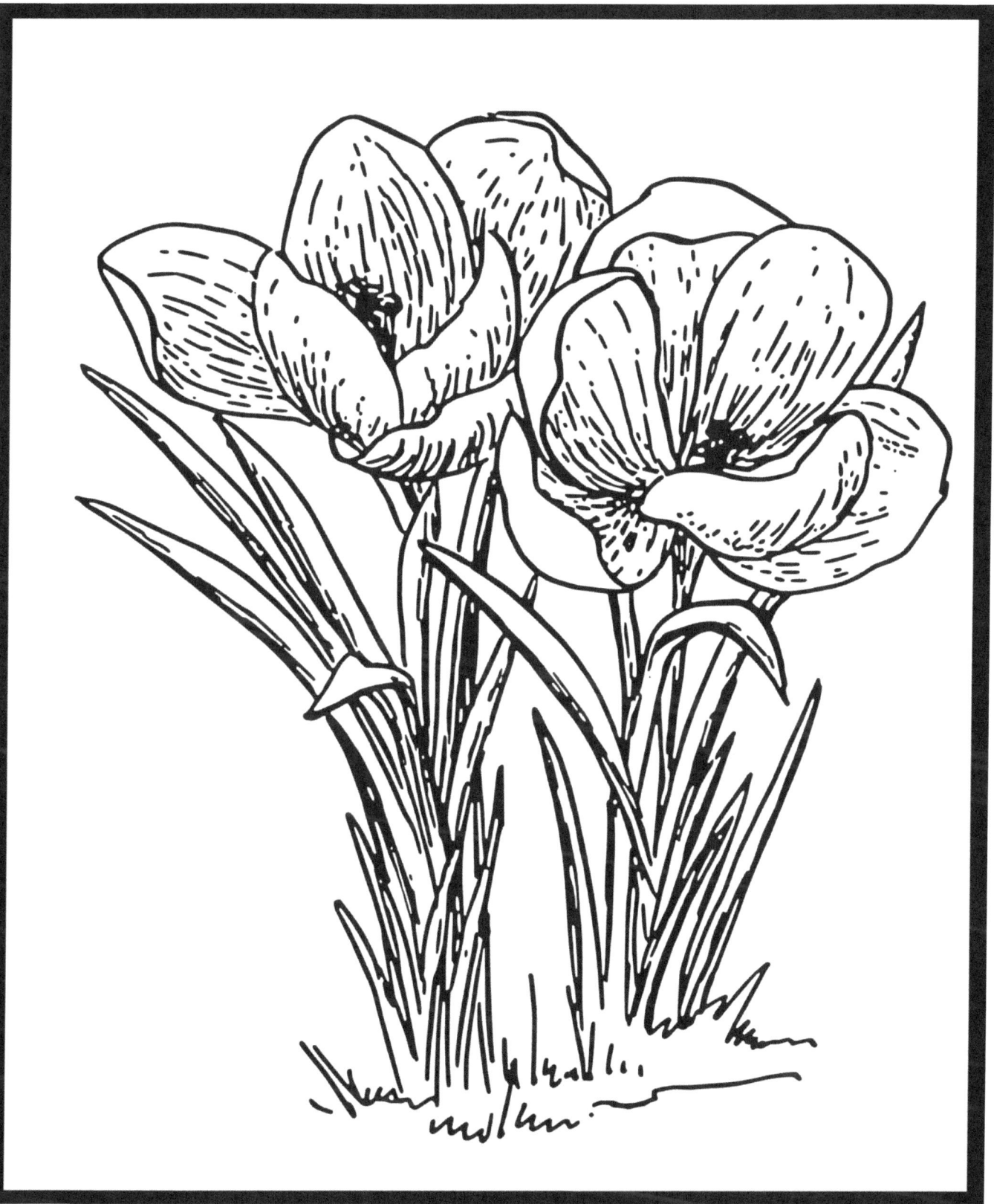

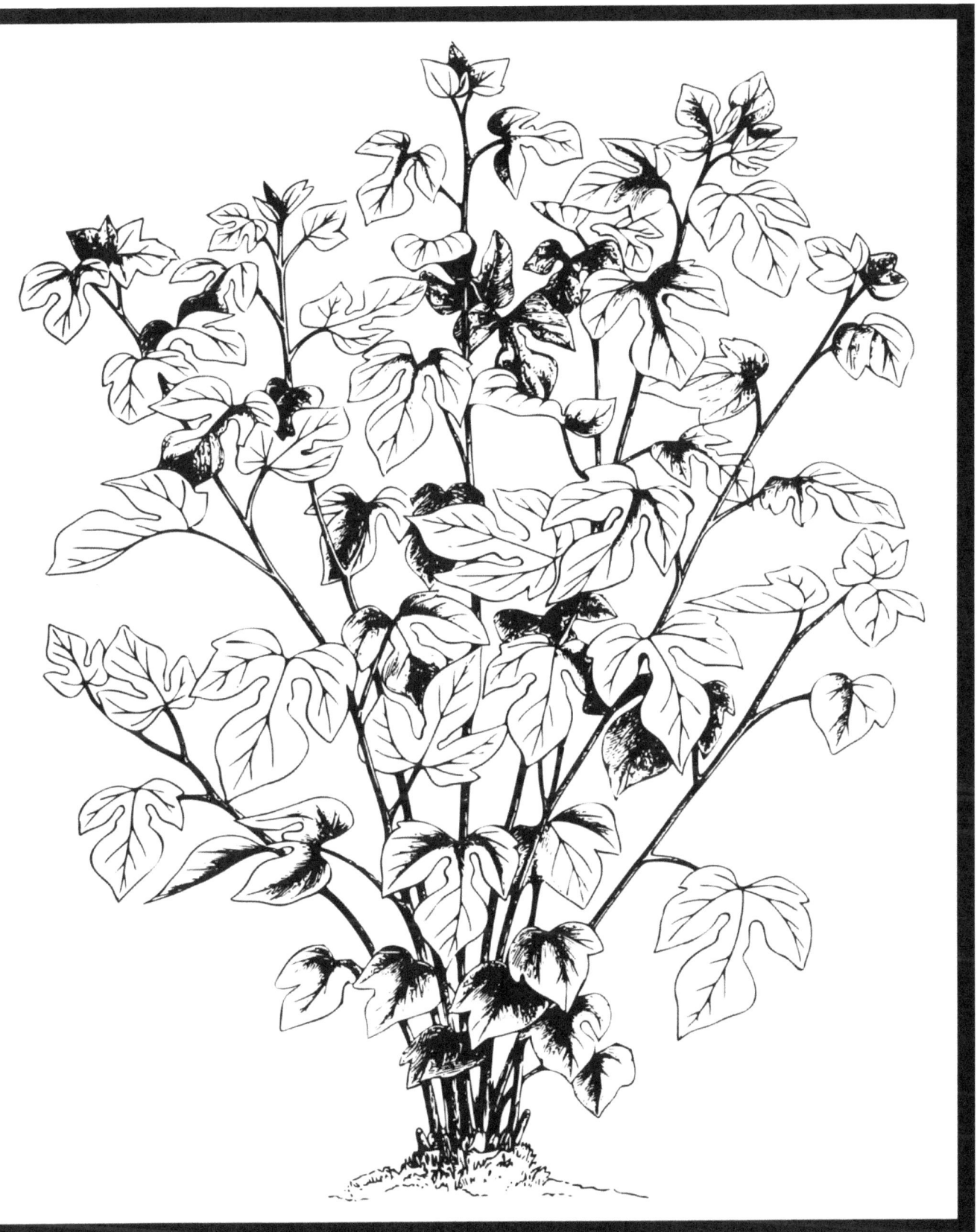

Floral Fantasies

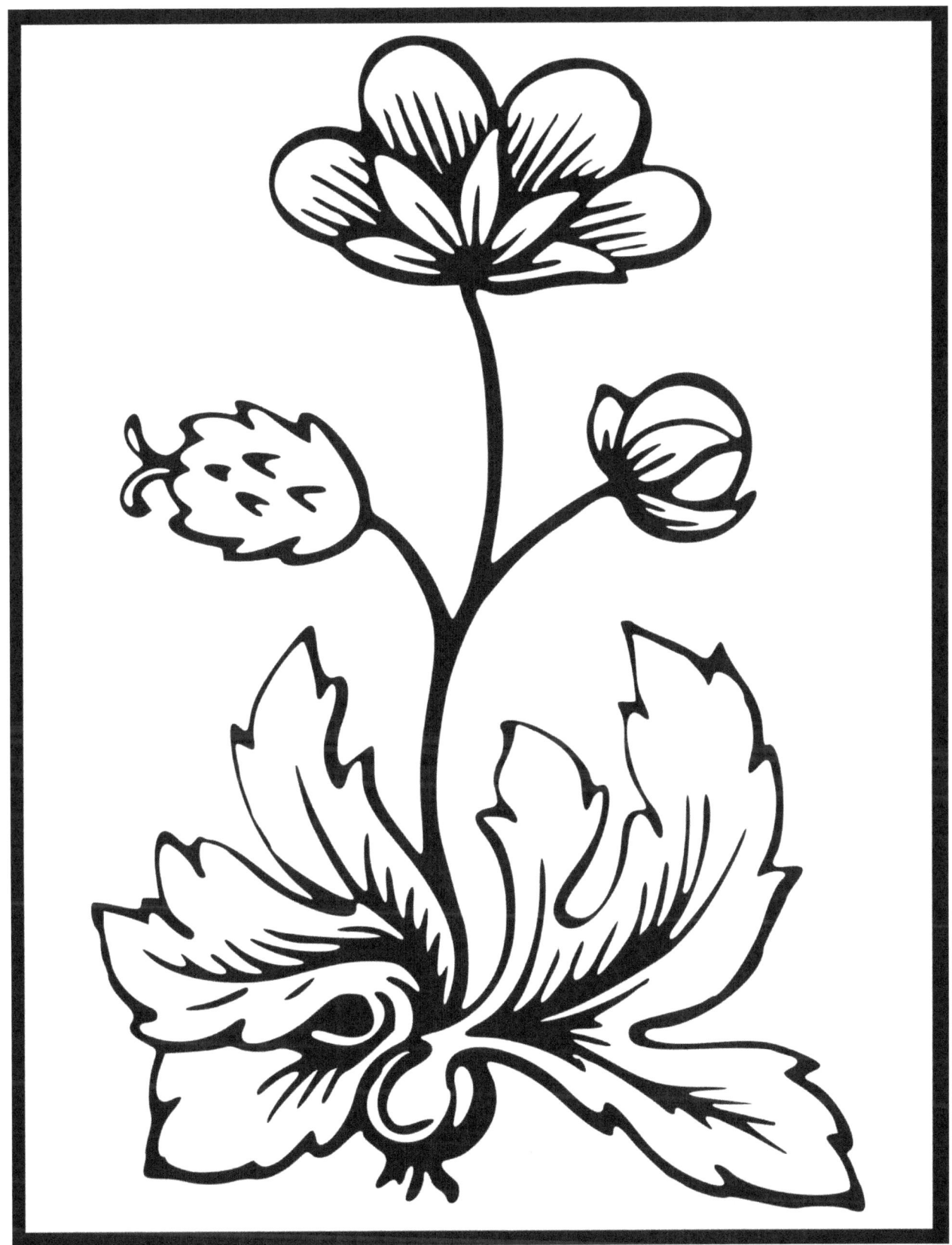

Floral Fantasies

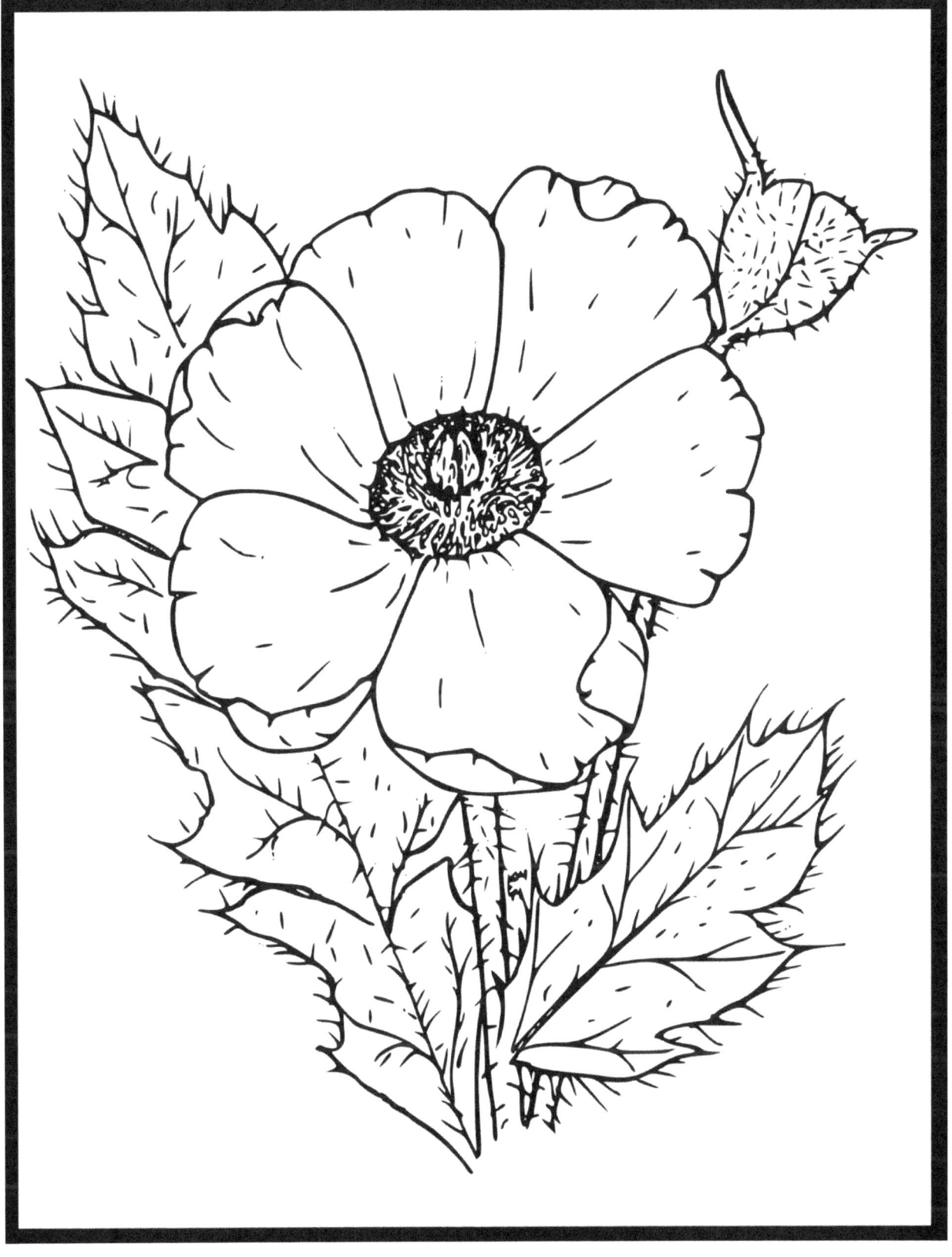

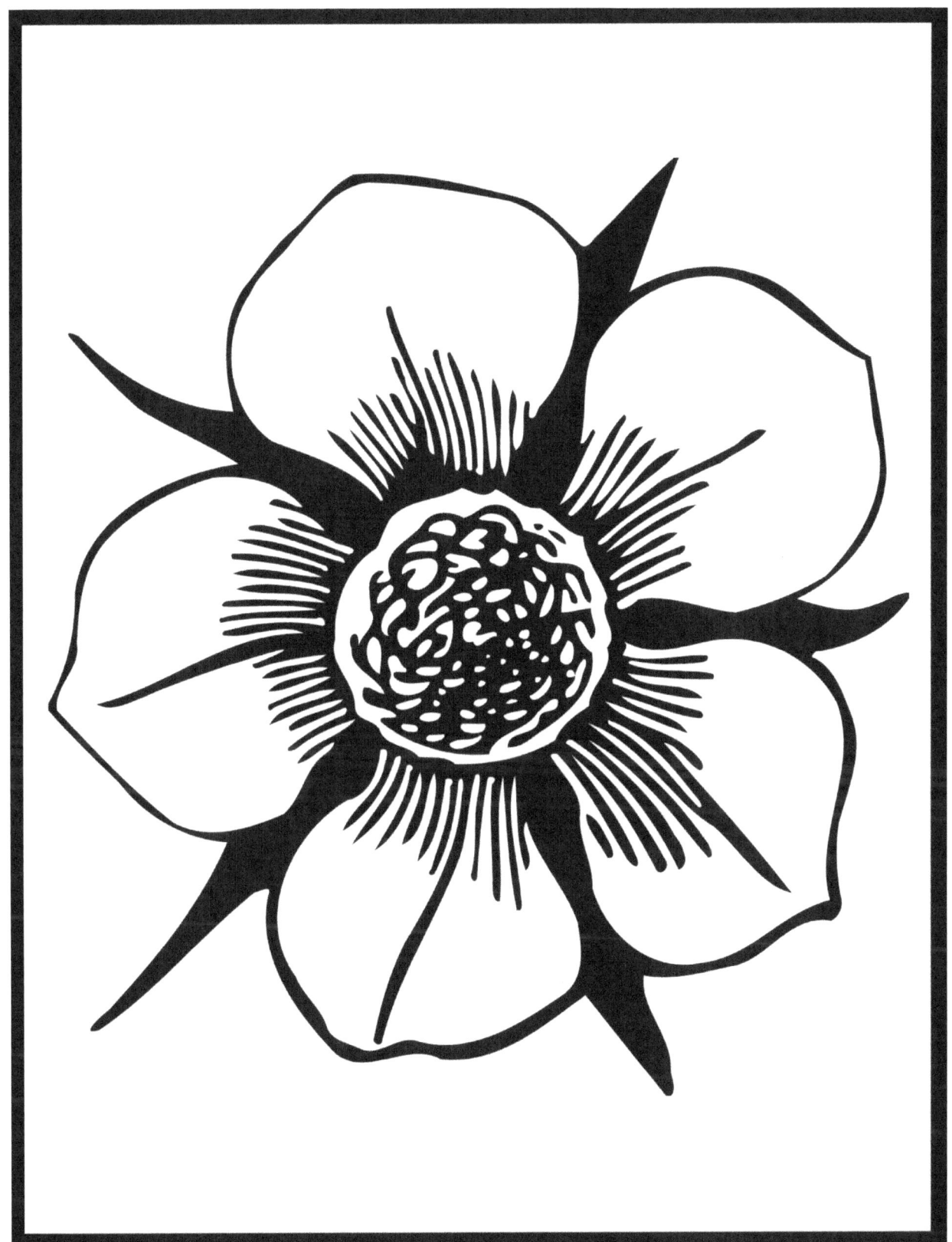

Floral Fantasies

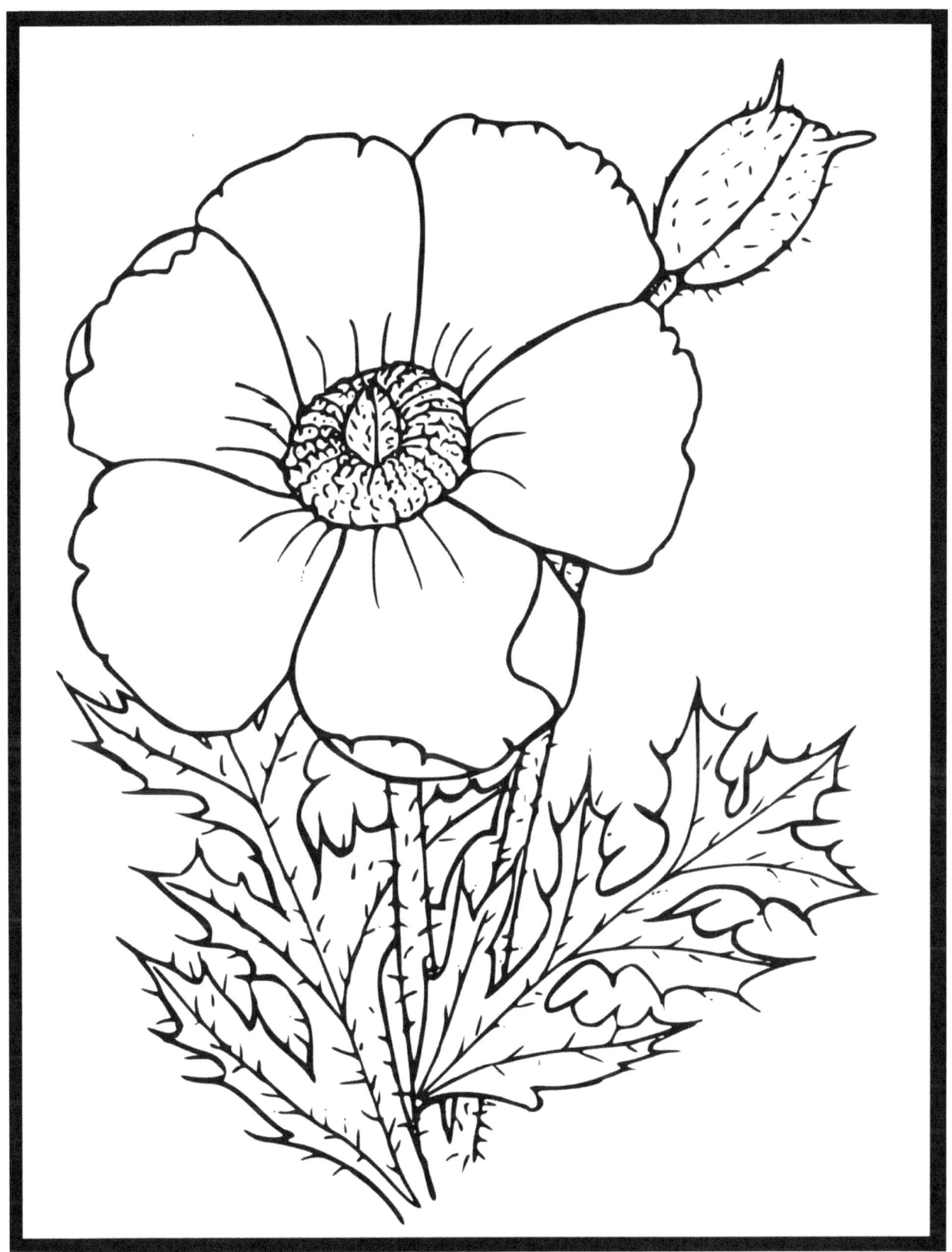

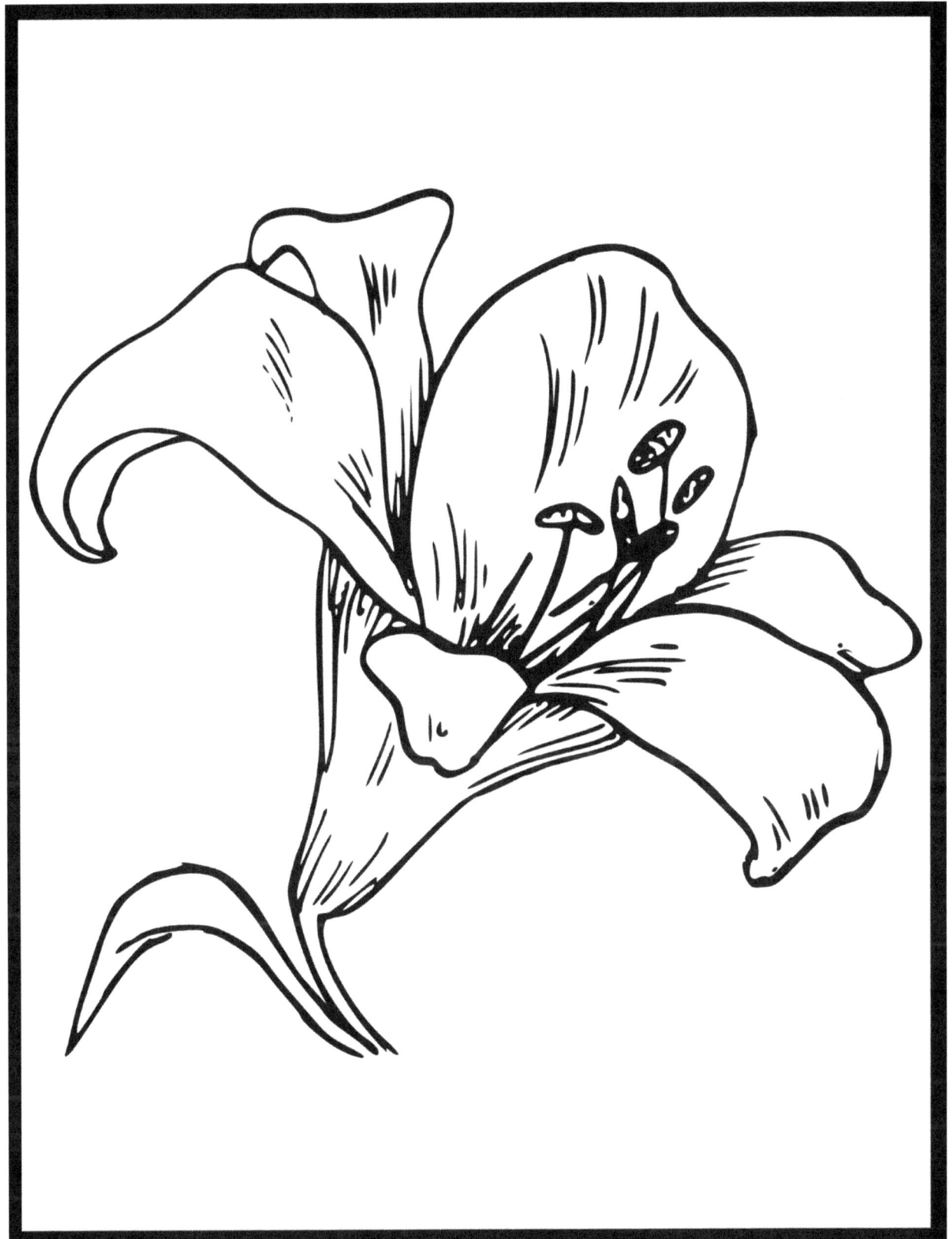

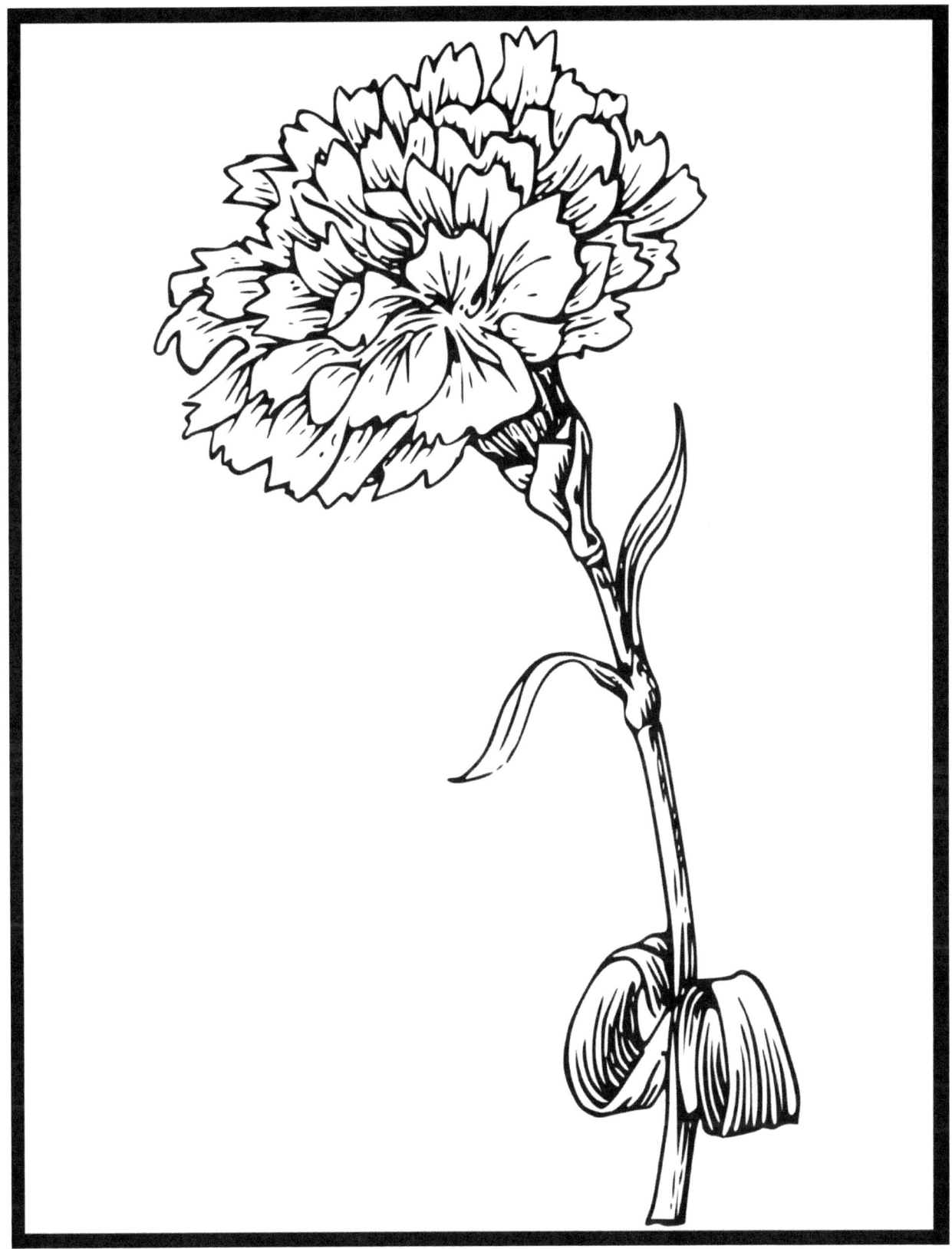

Floral Fantasies

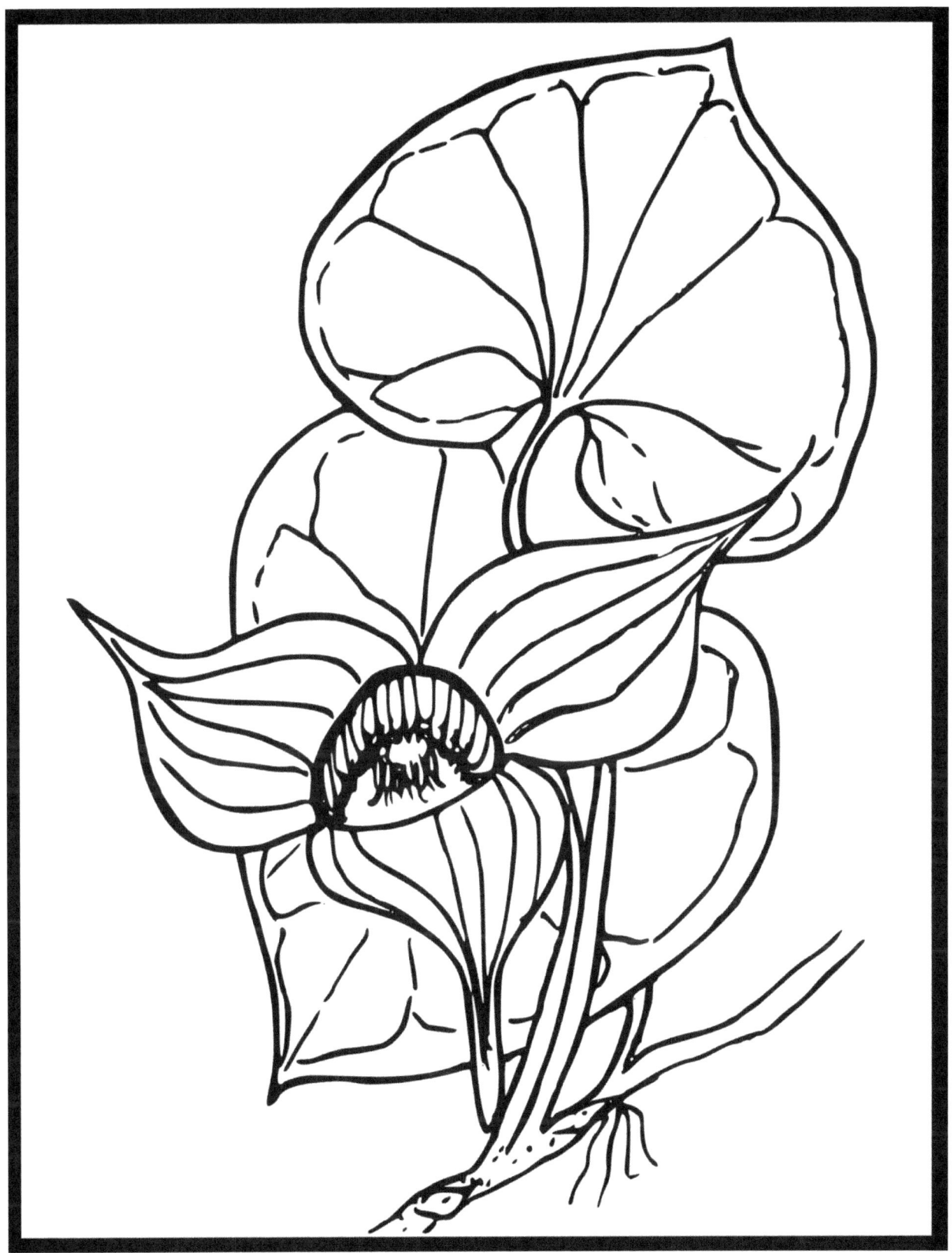

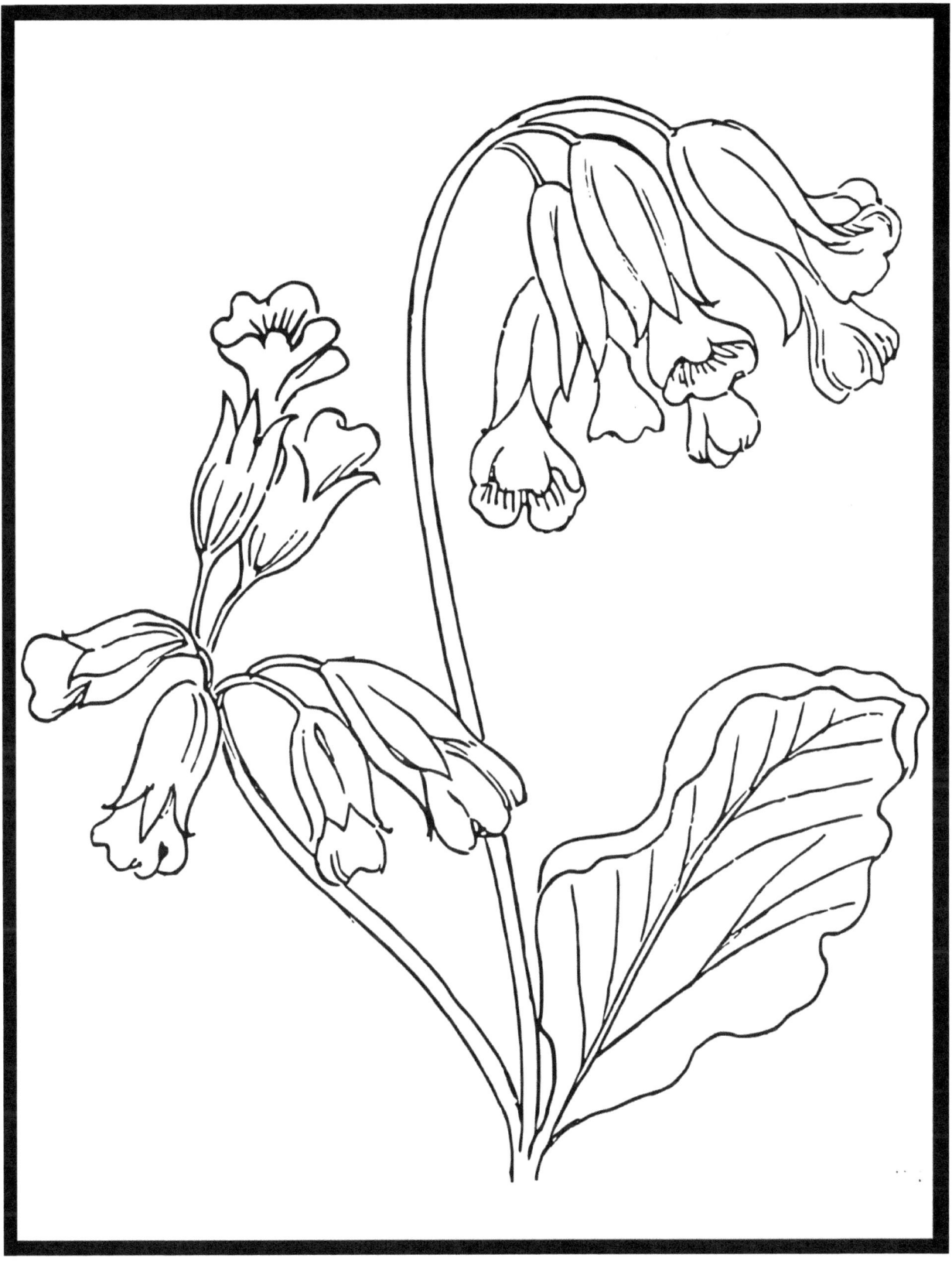

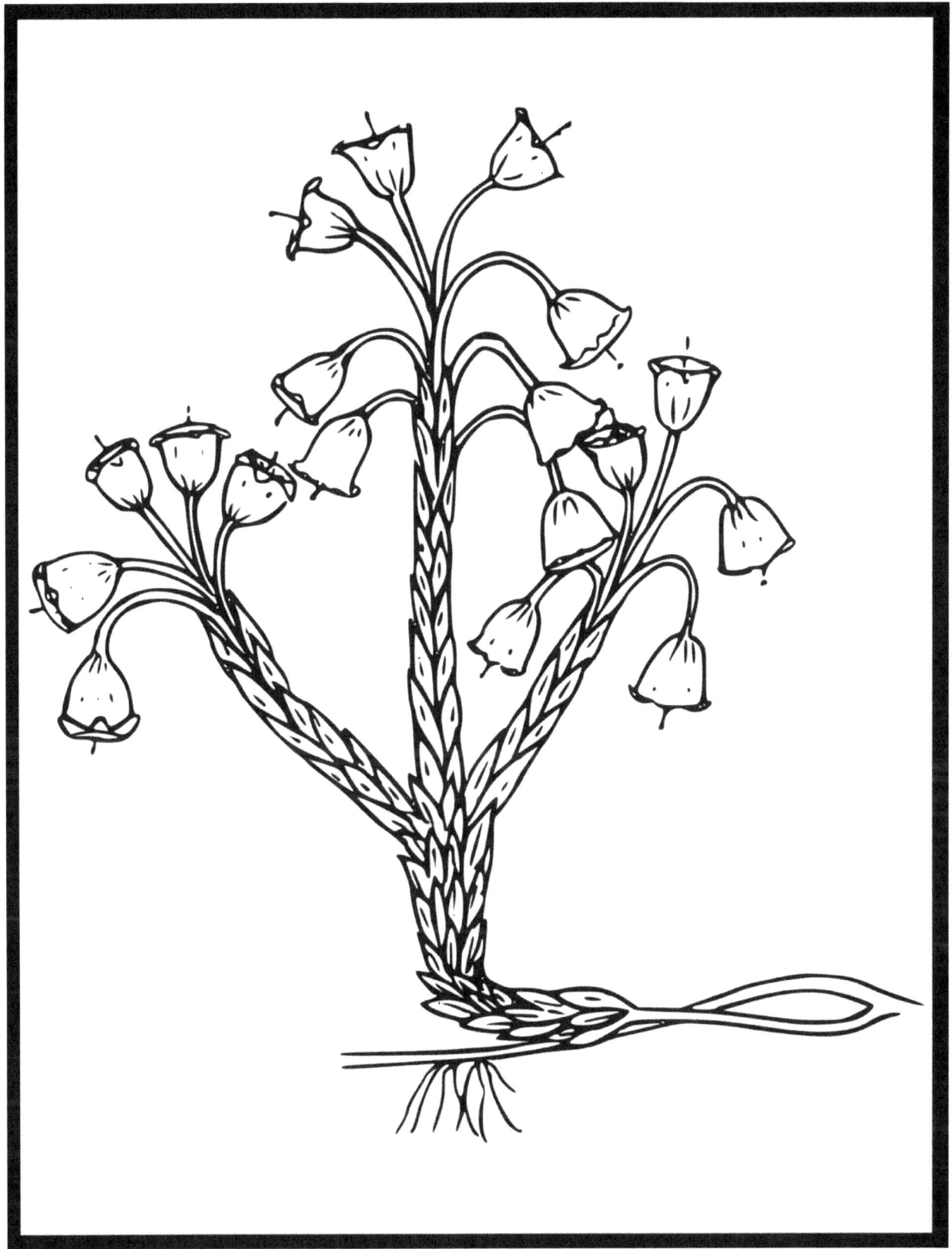

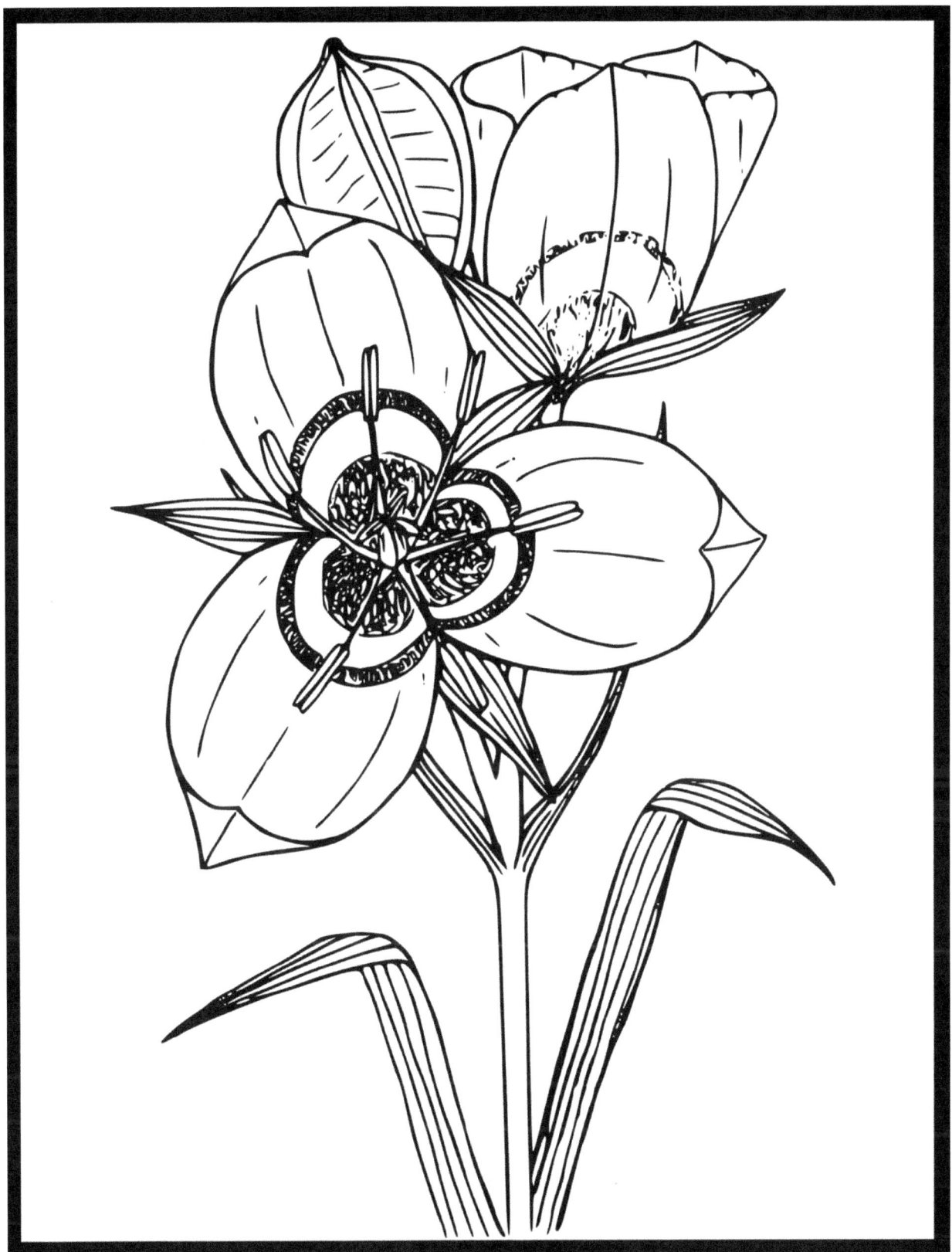

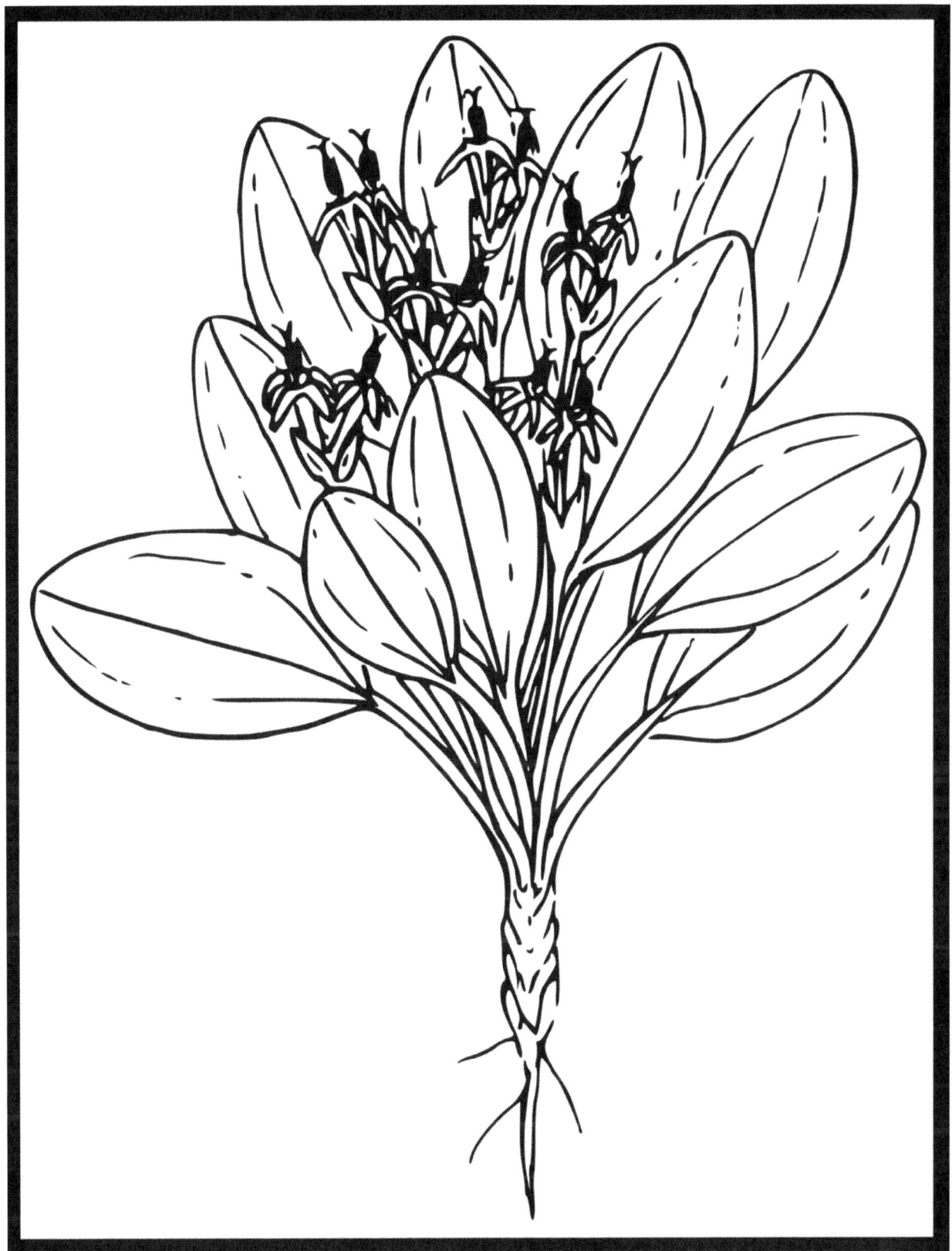

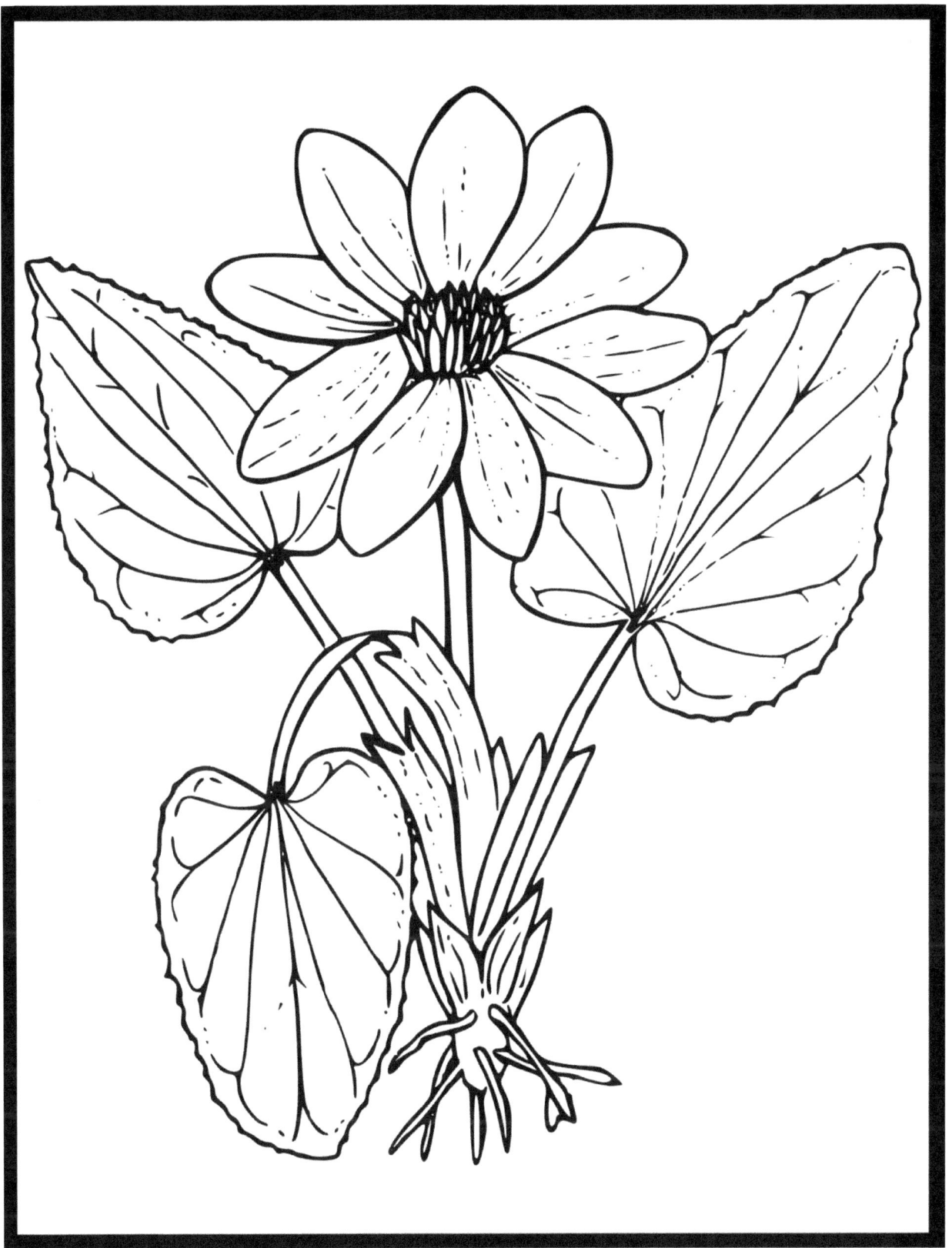

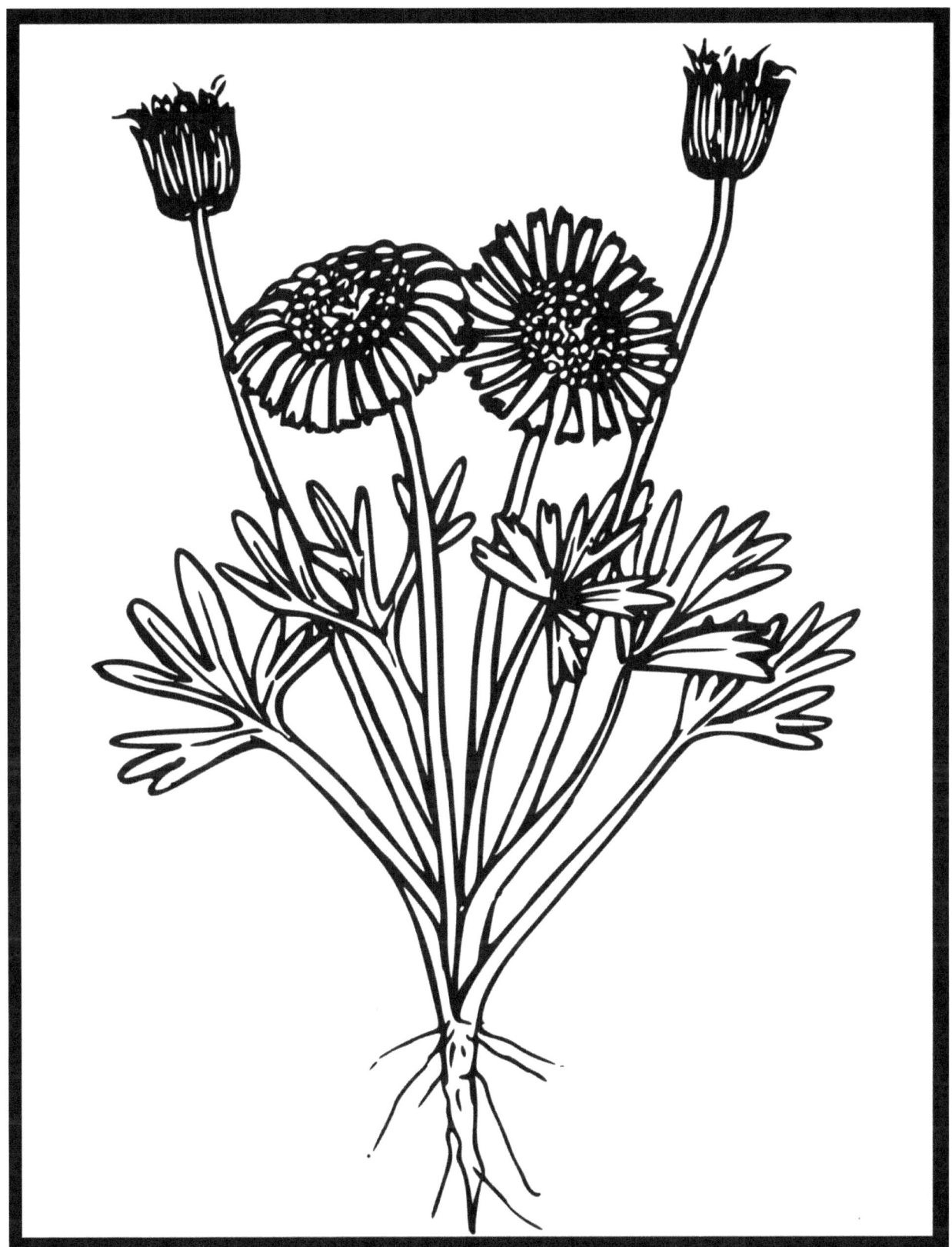

Floral Fantasies

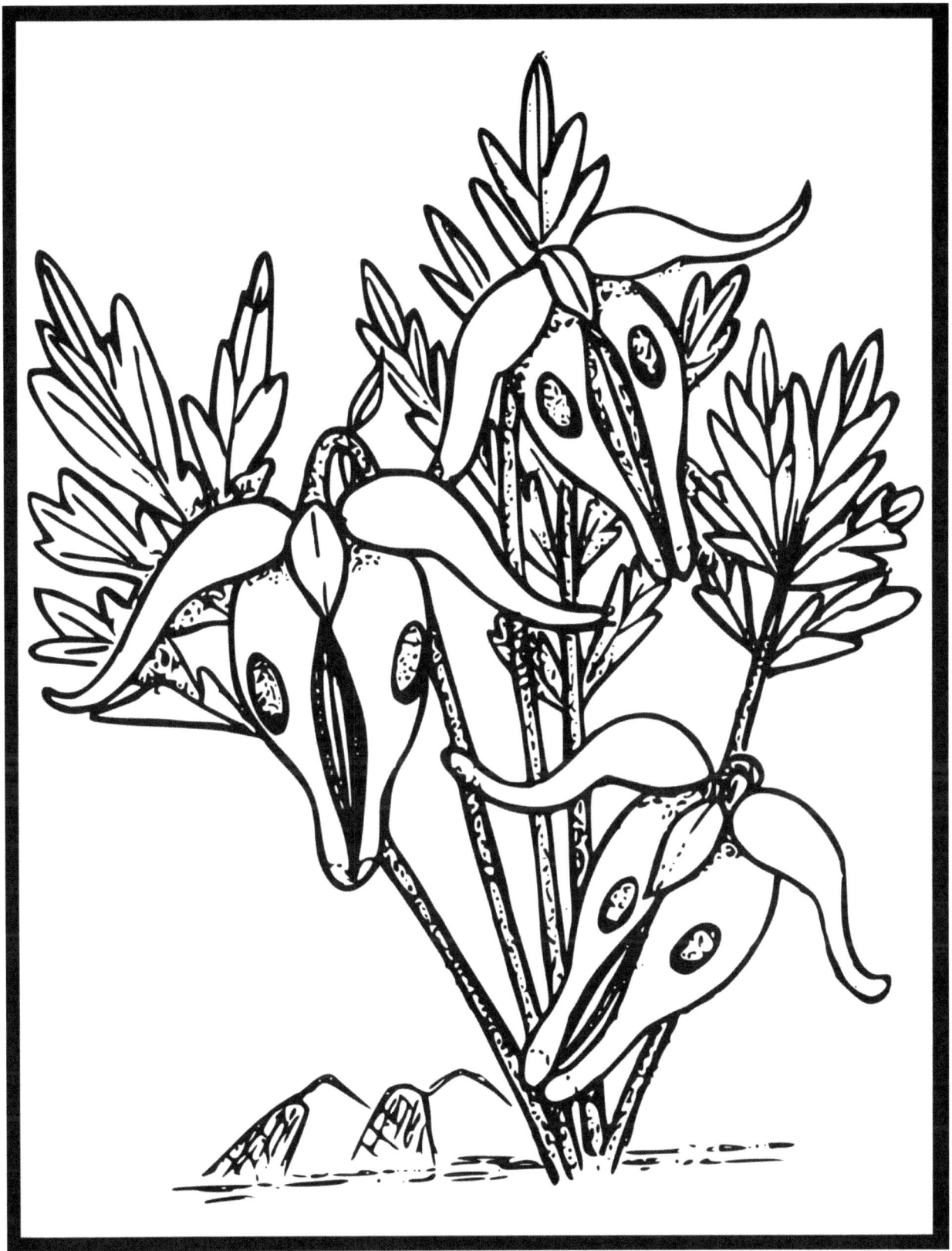

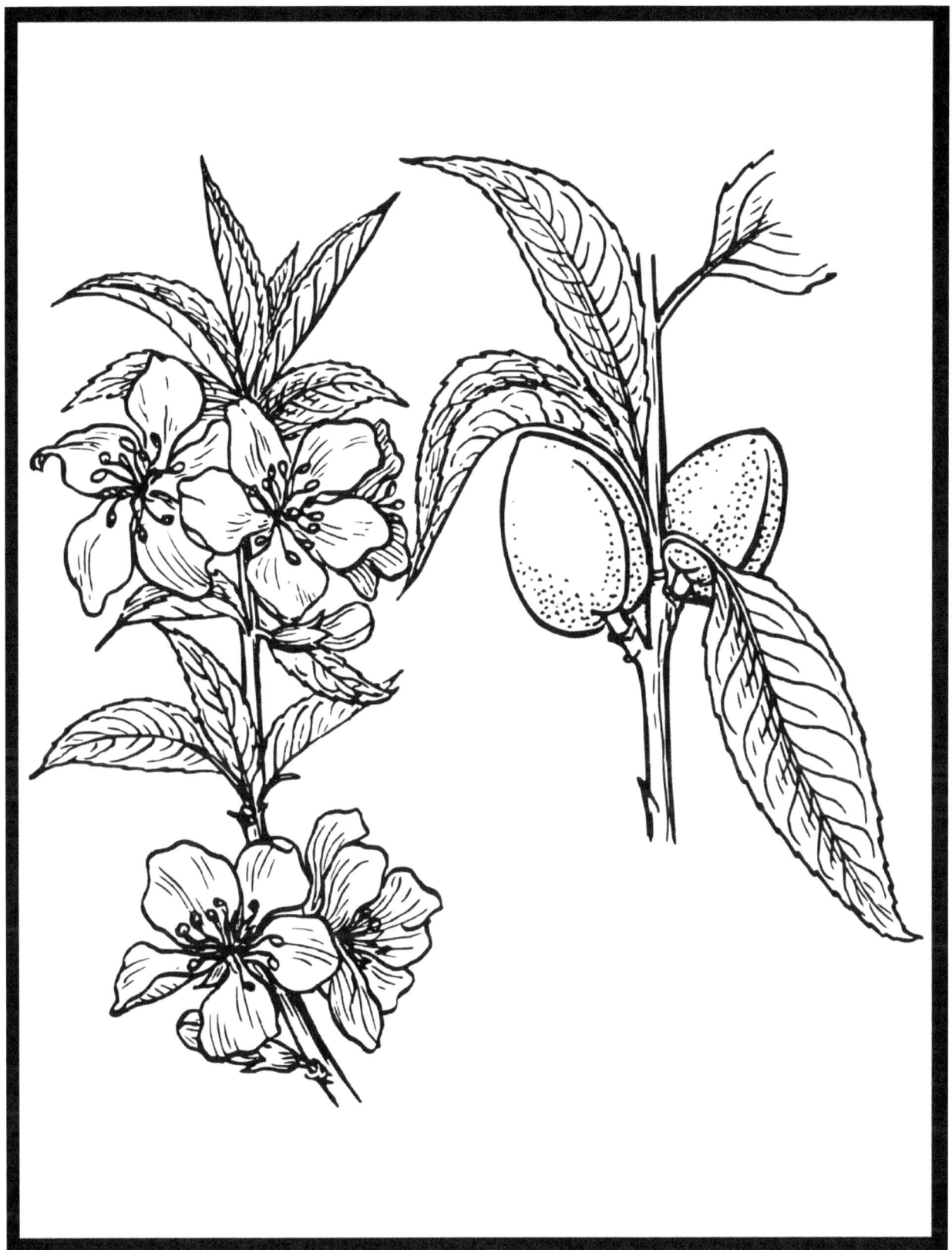

Floral Fantasies

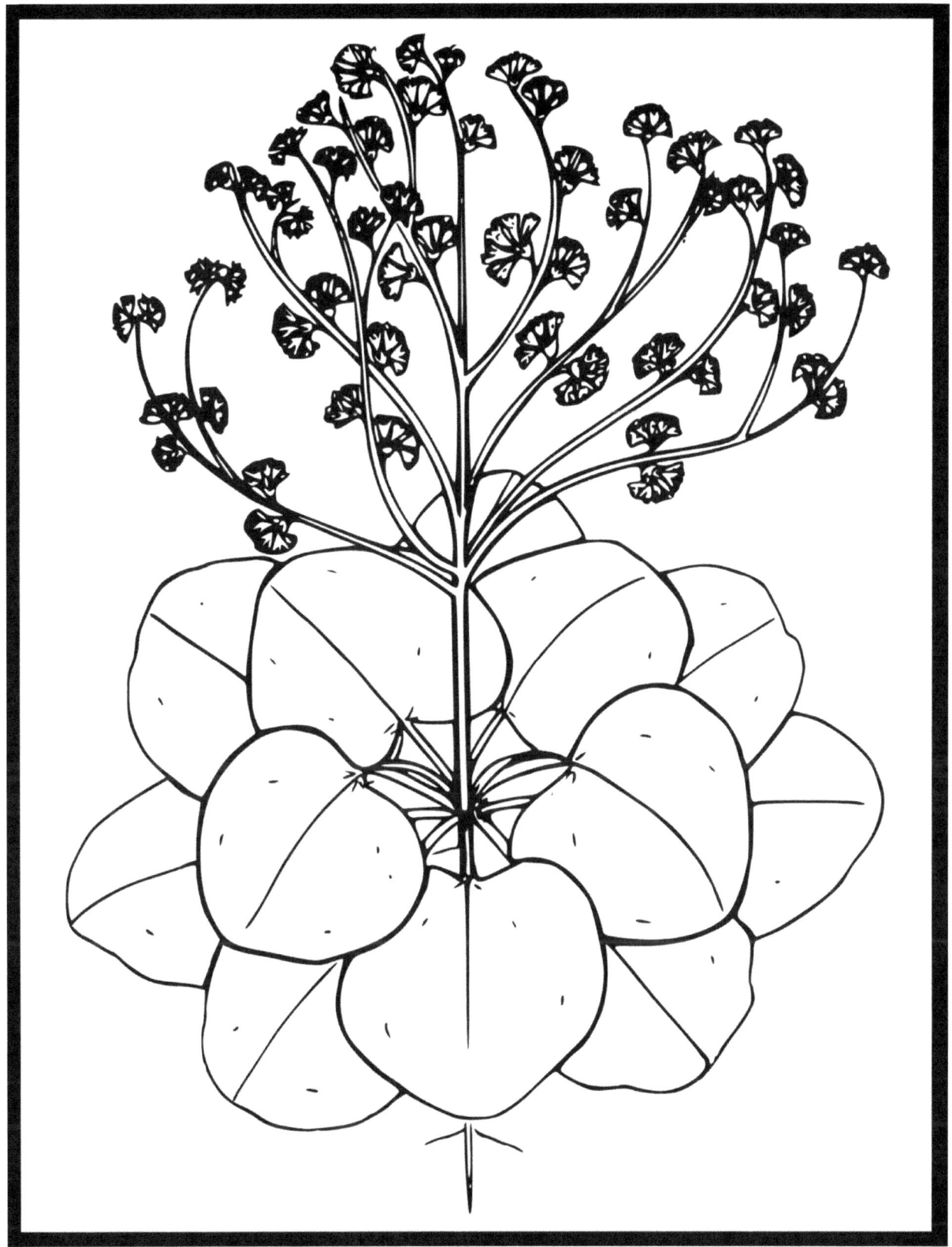

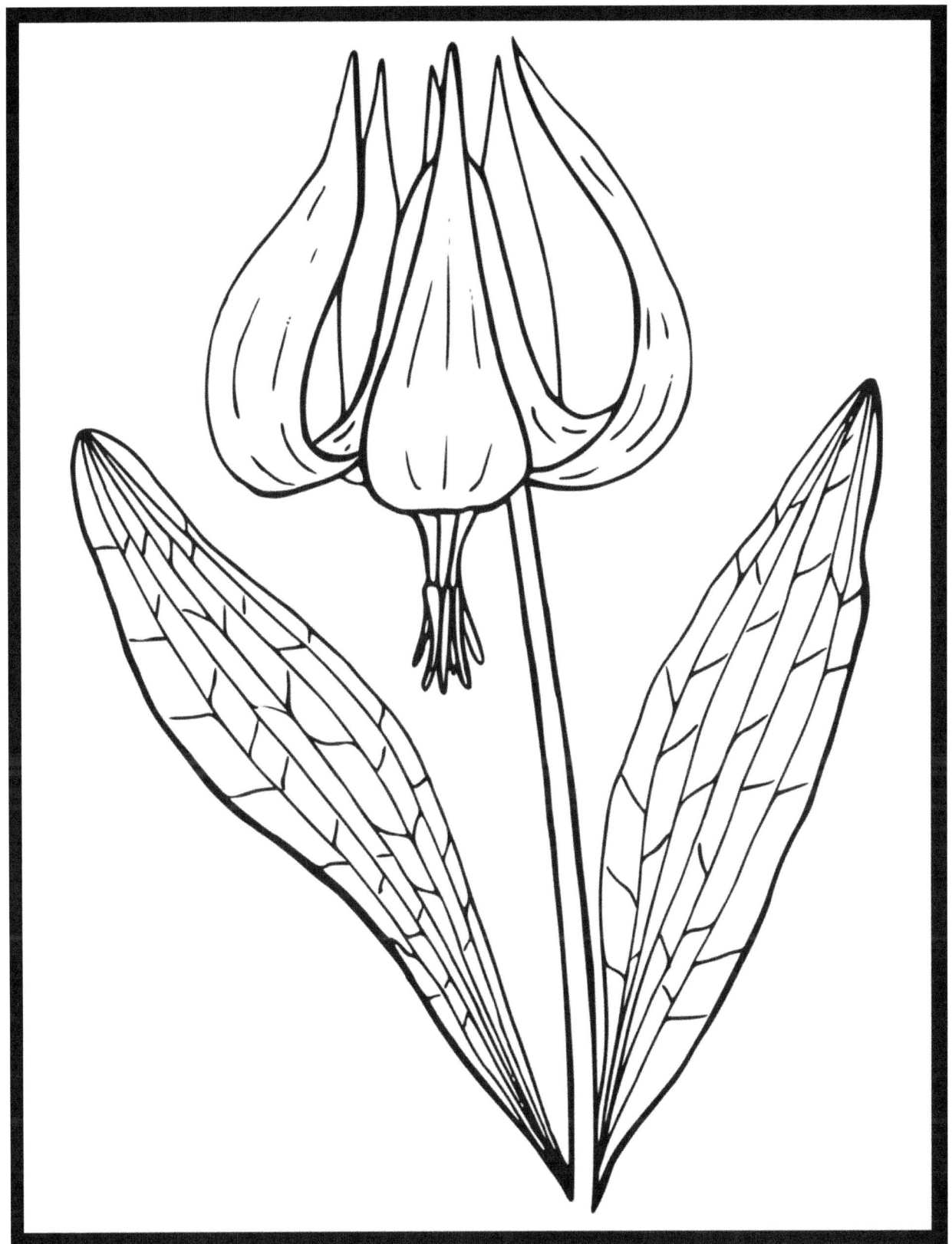

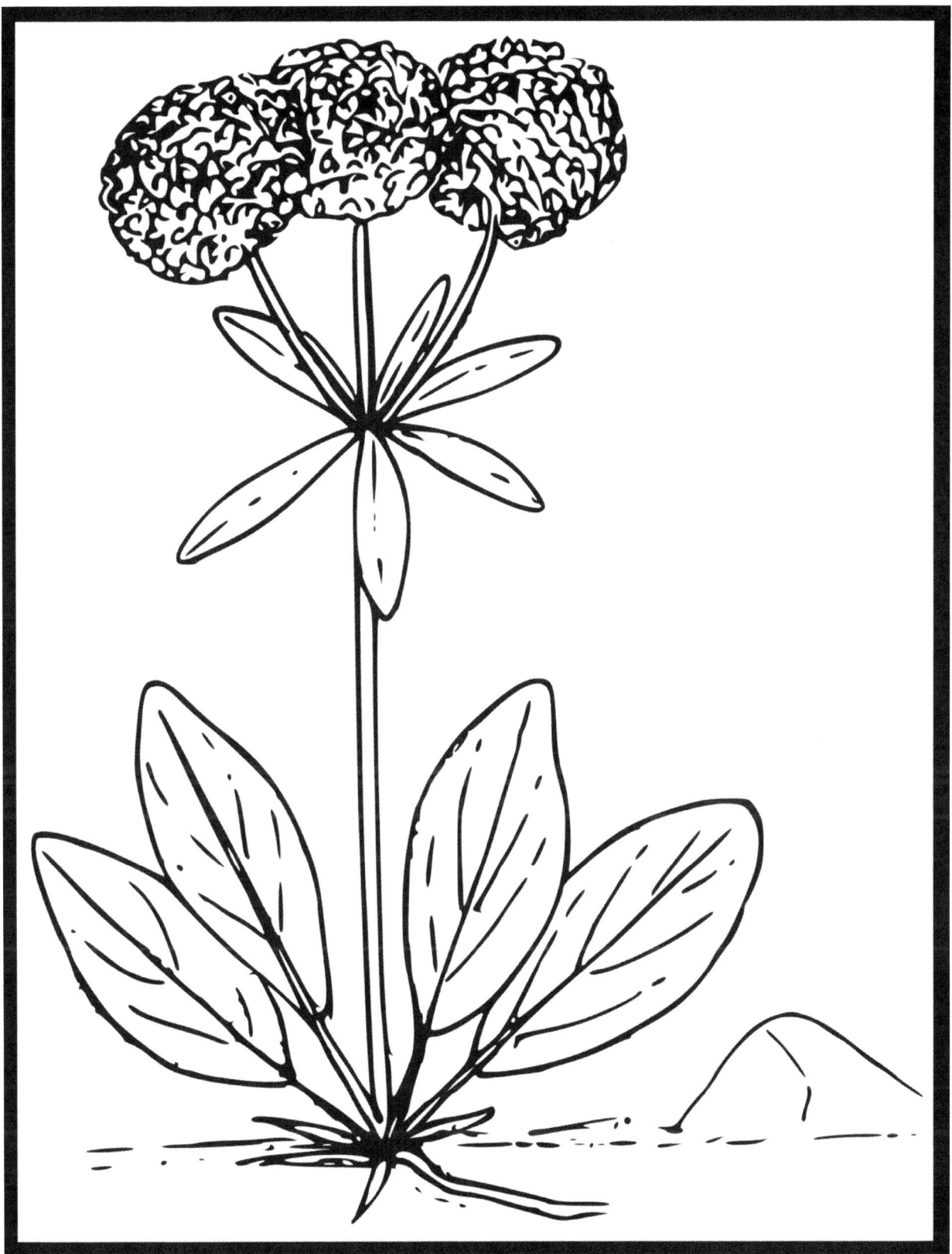

Floral Fantasies

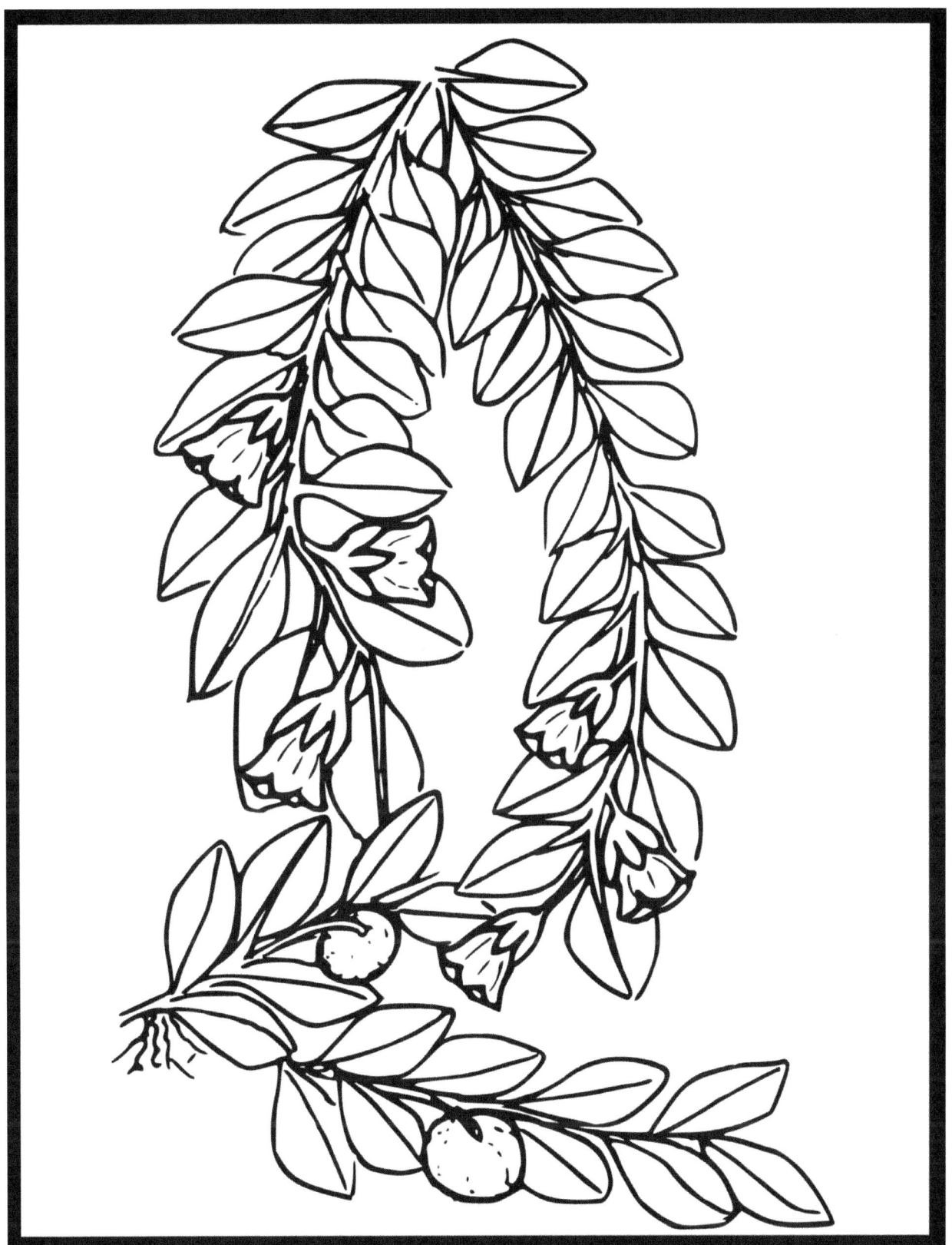

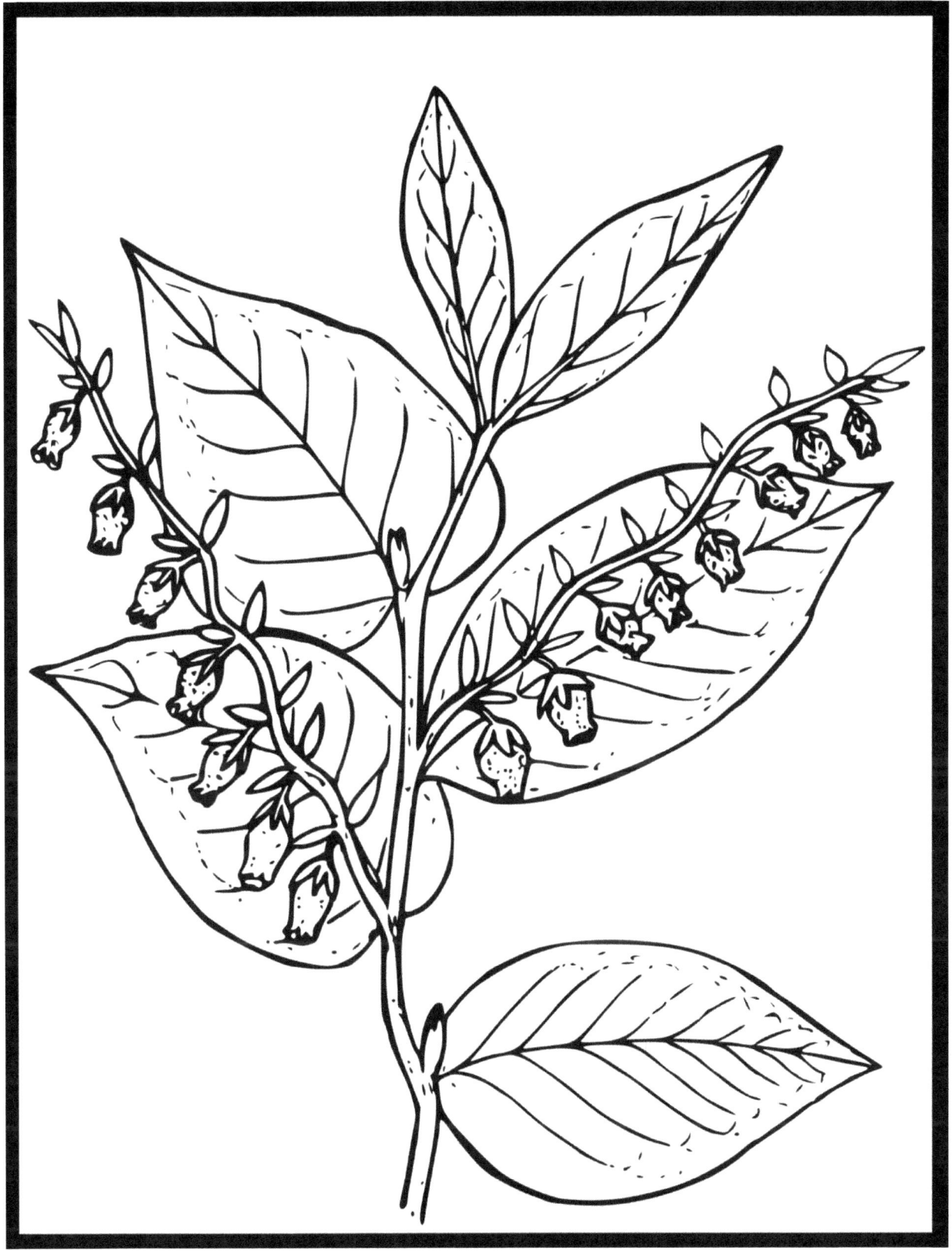

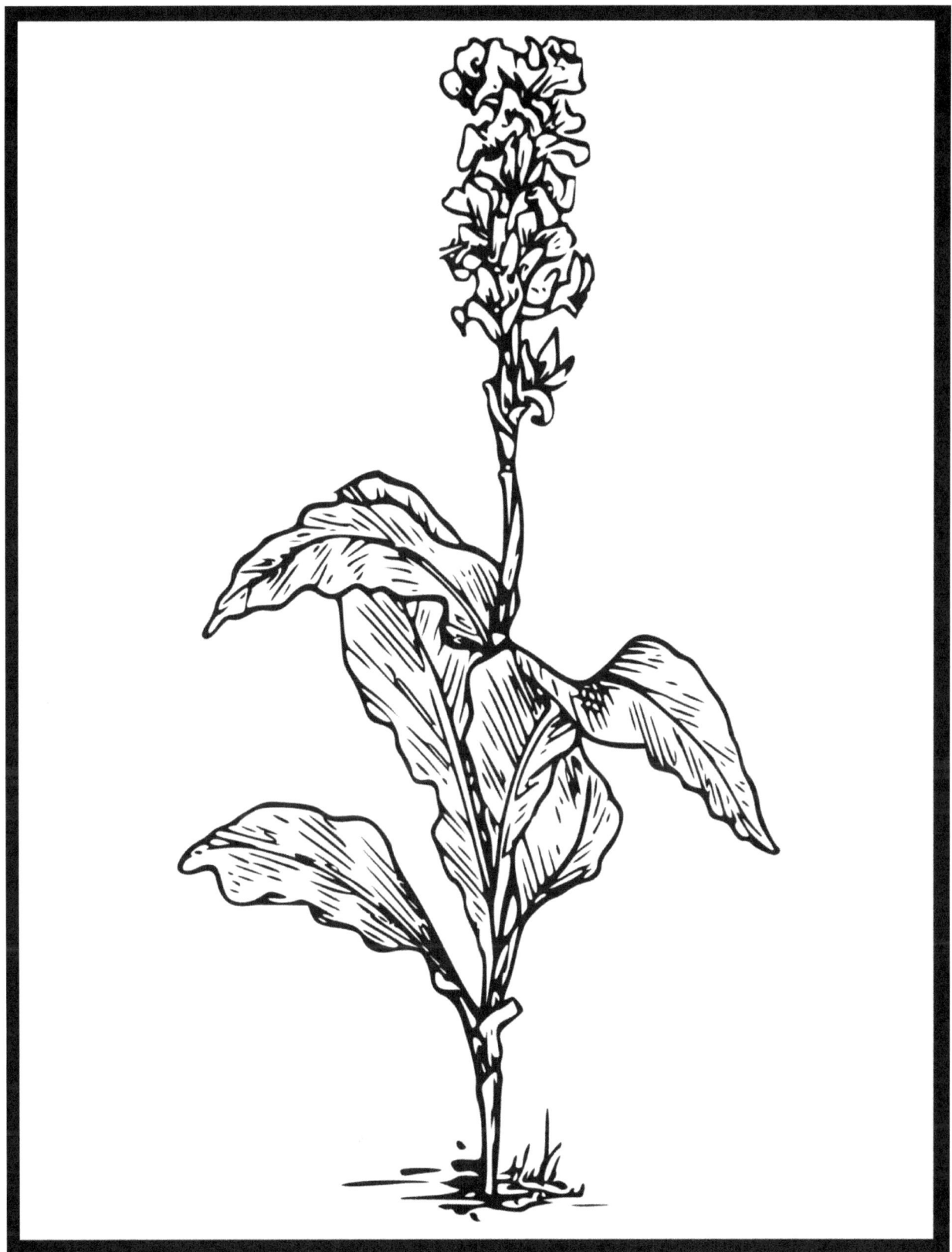

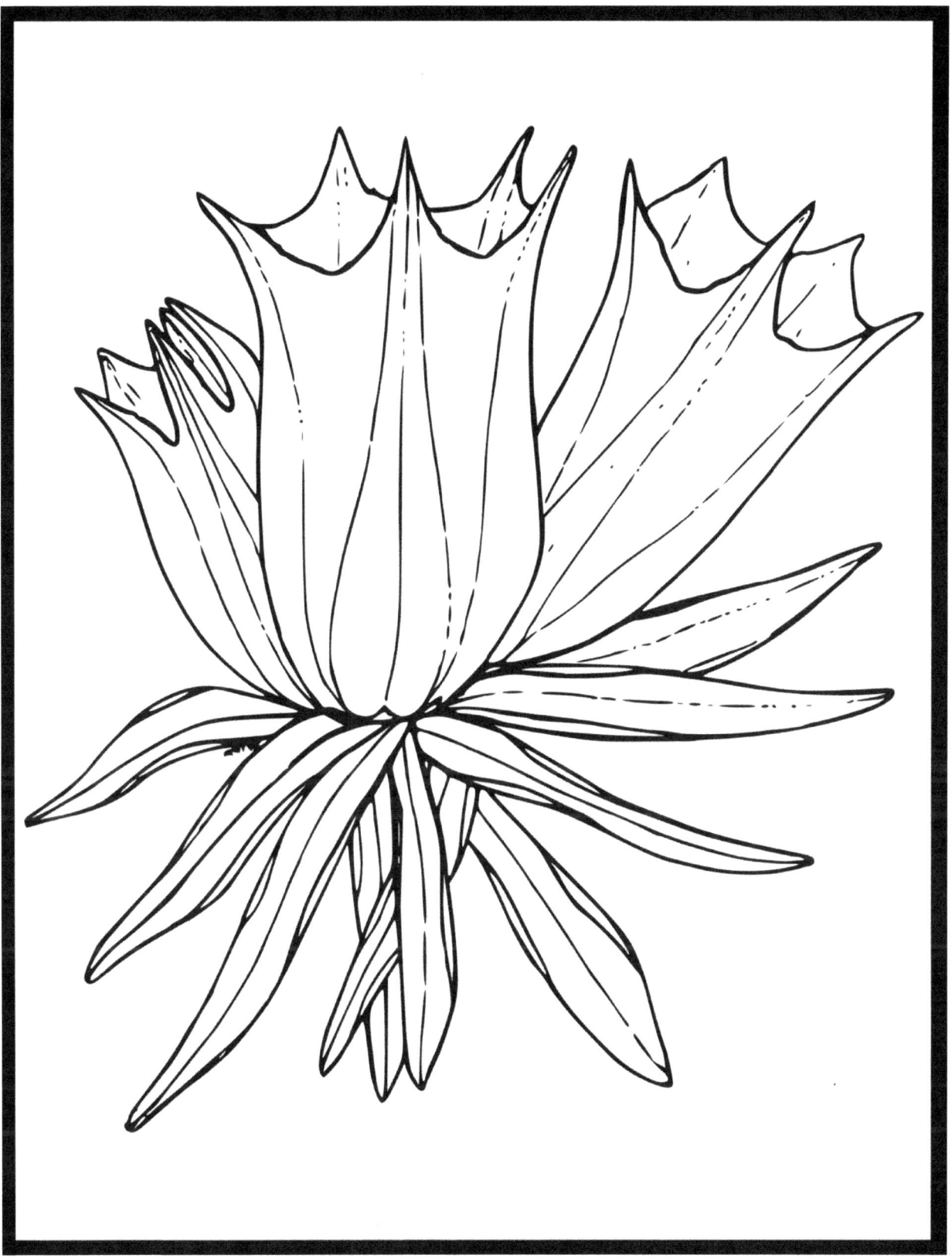

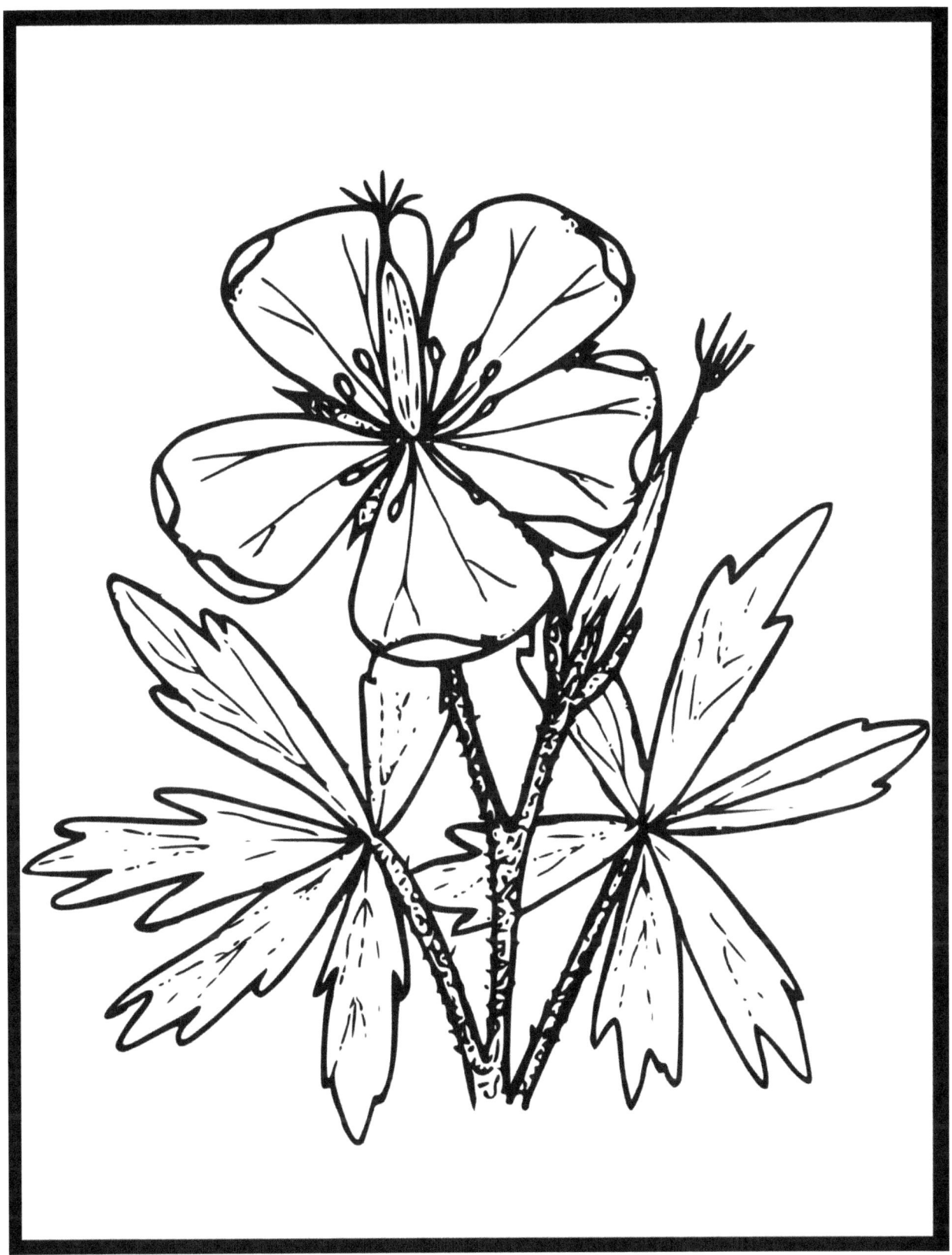

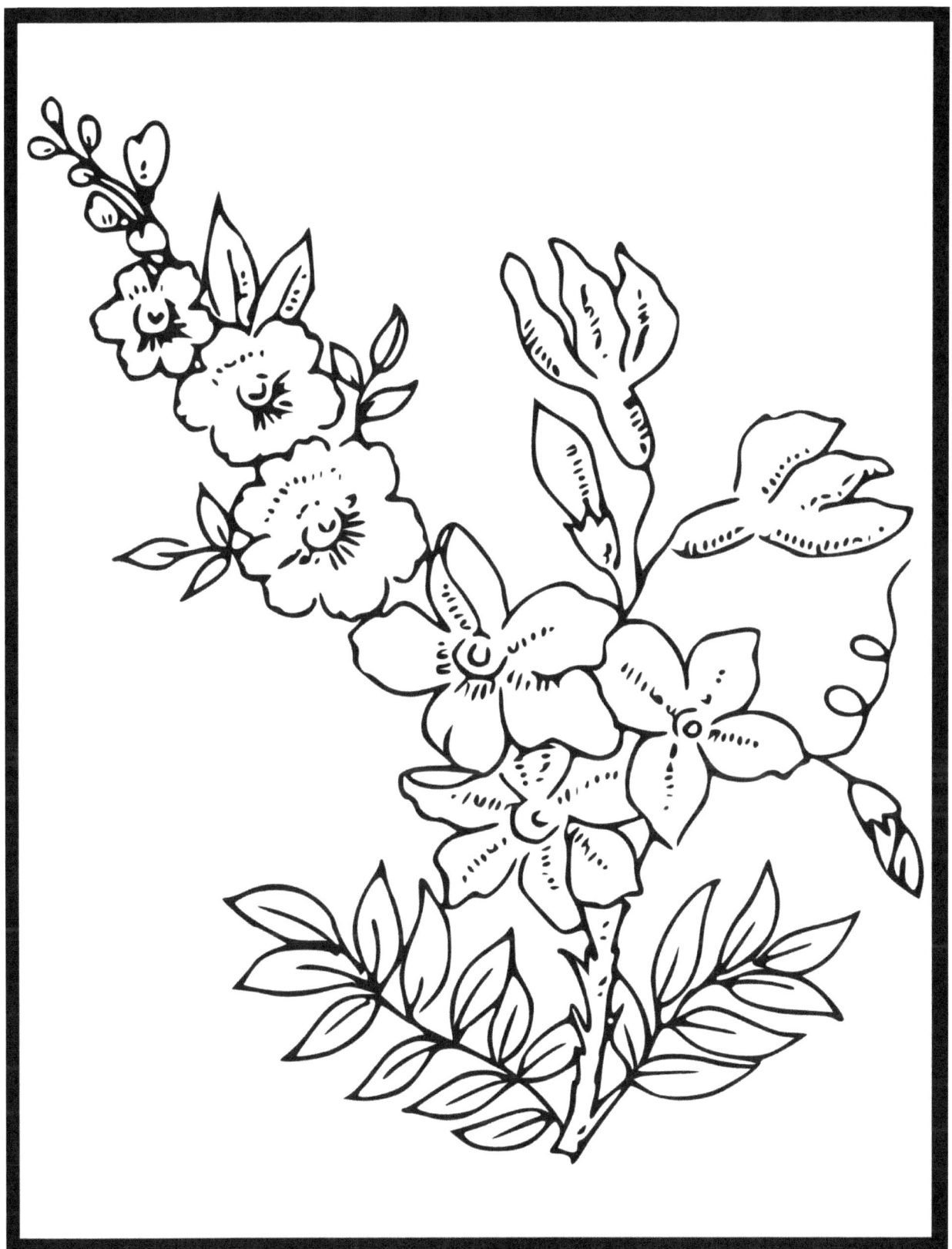

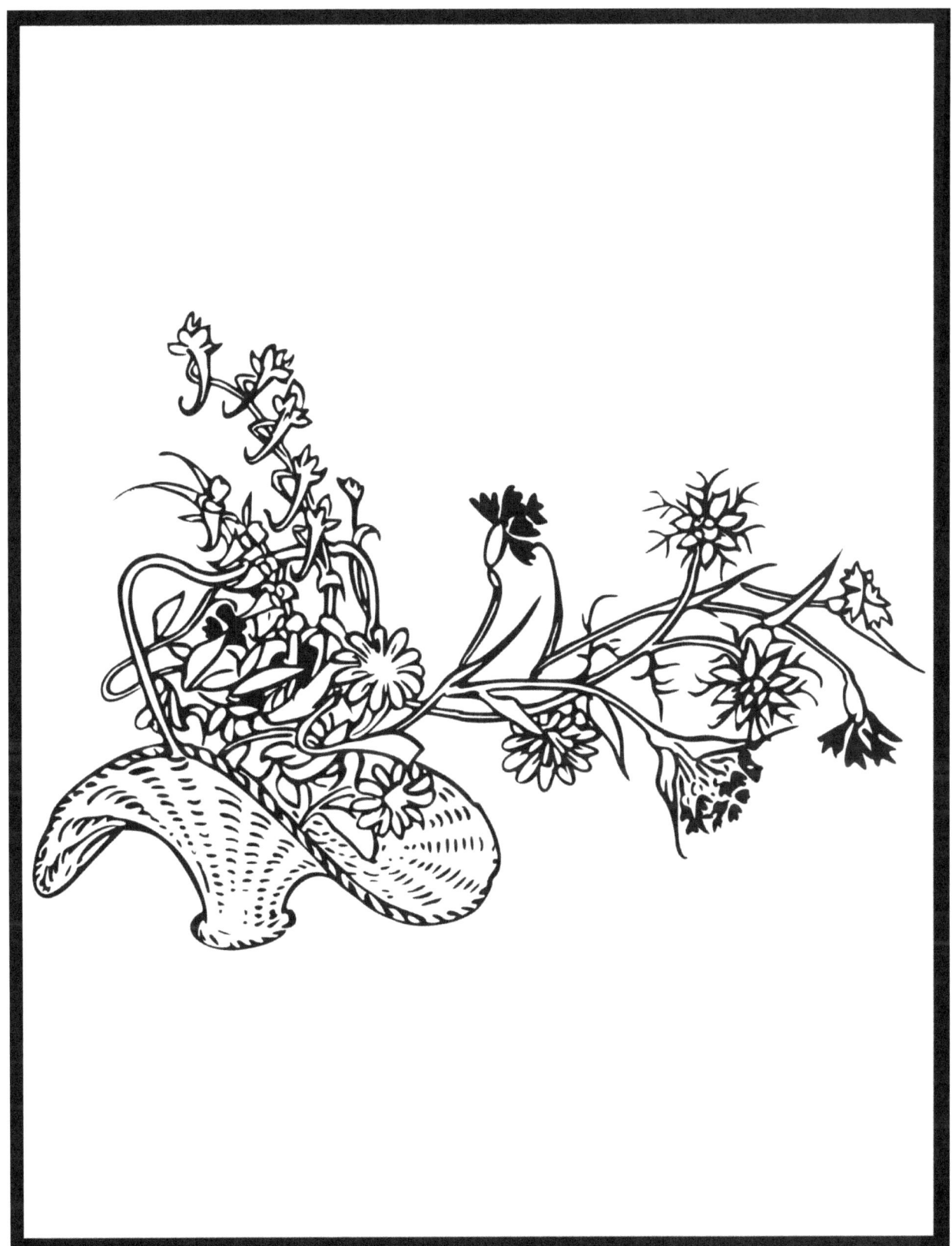

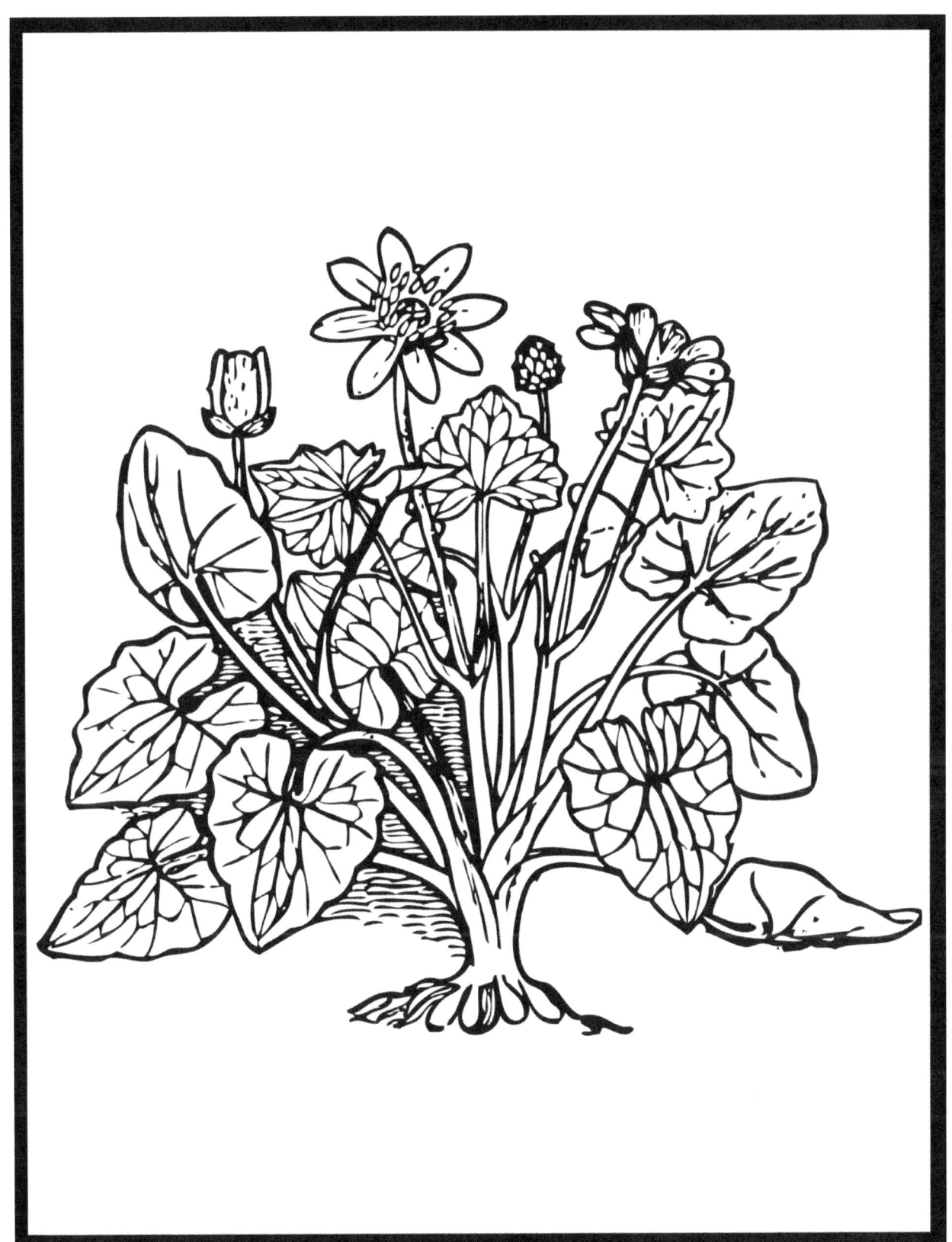

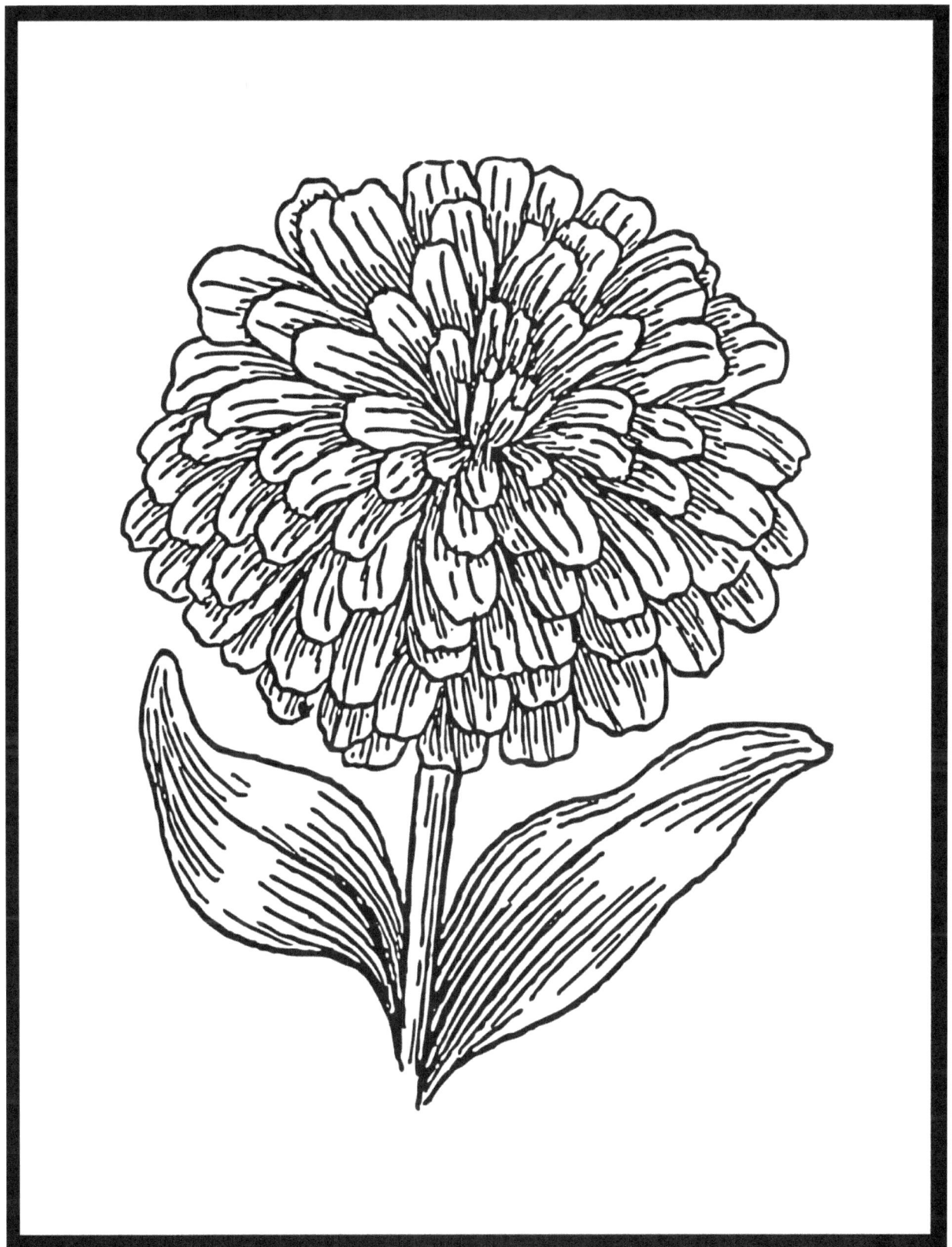

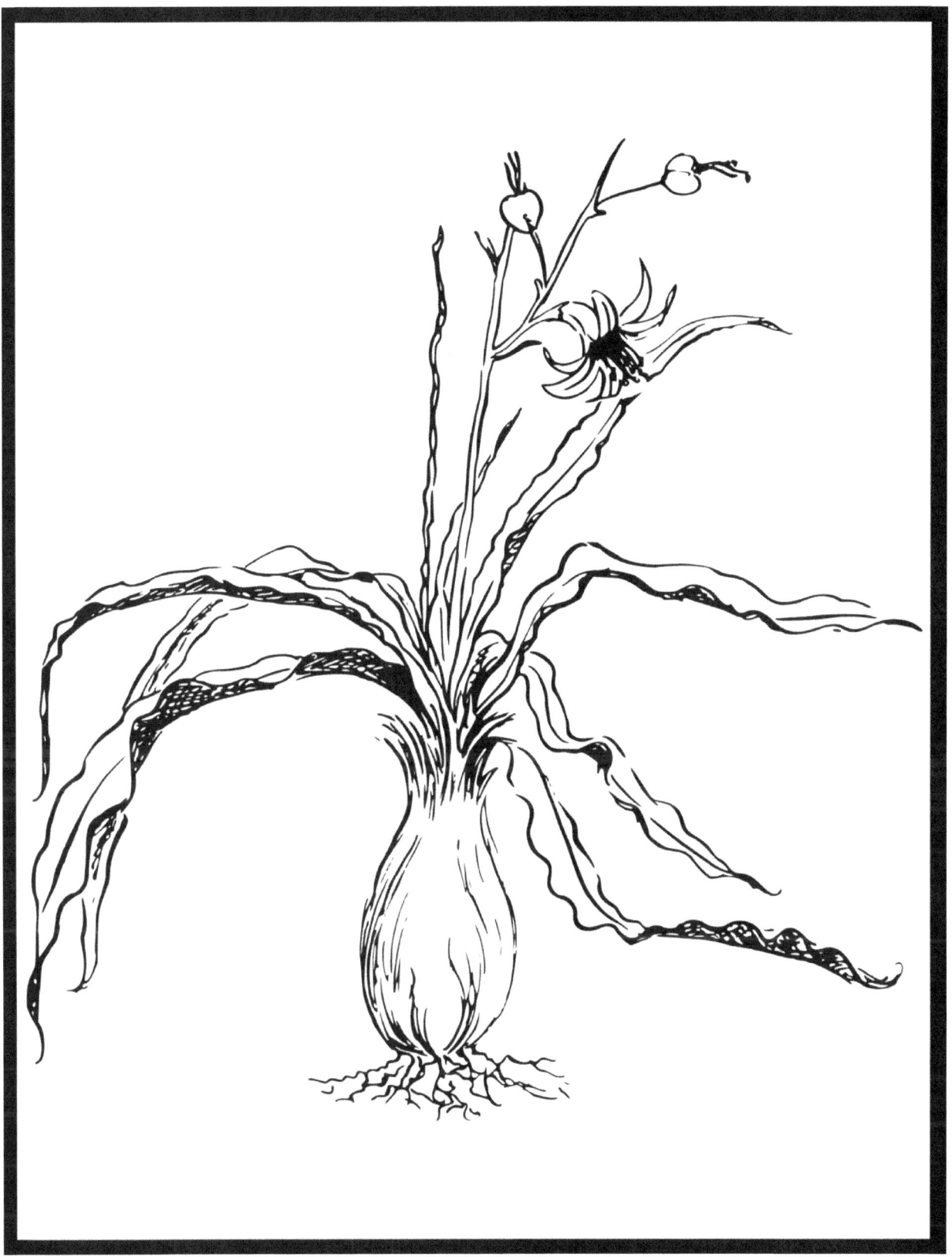

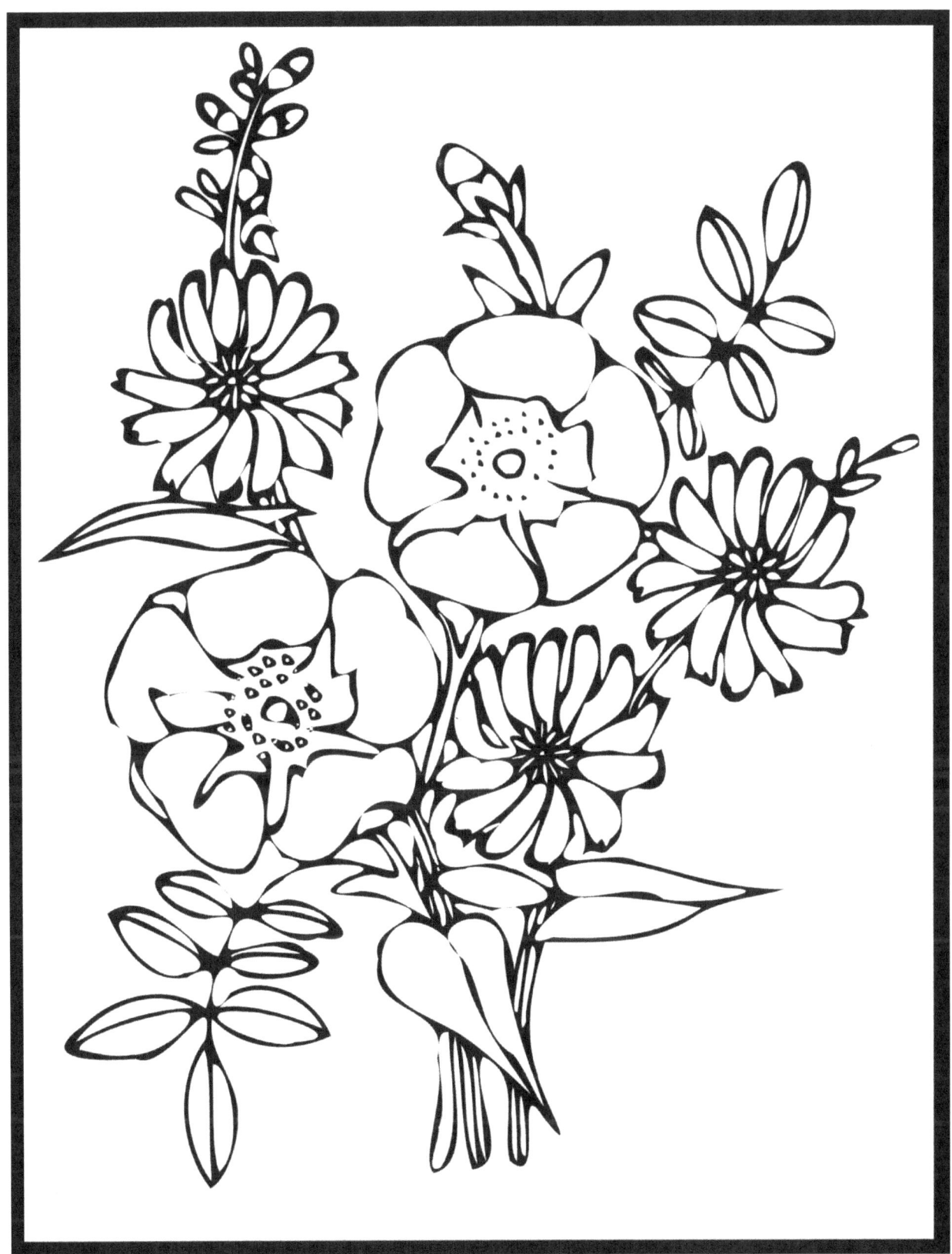

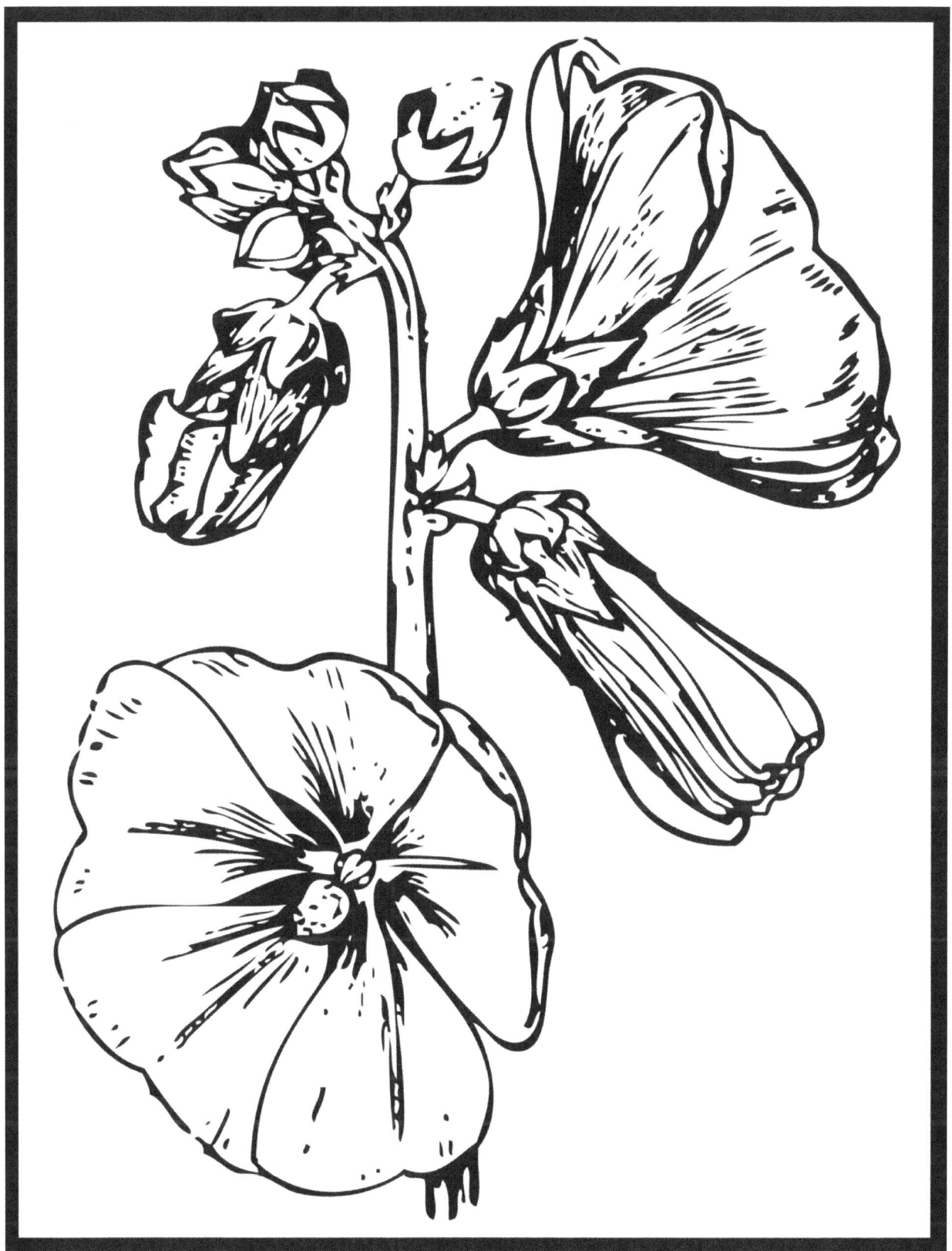

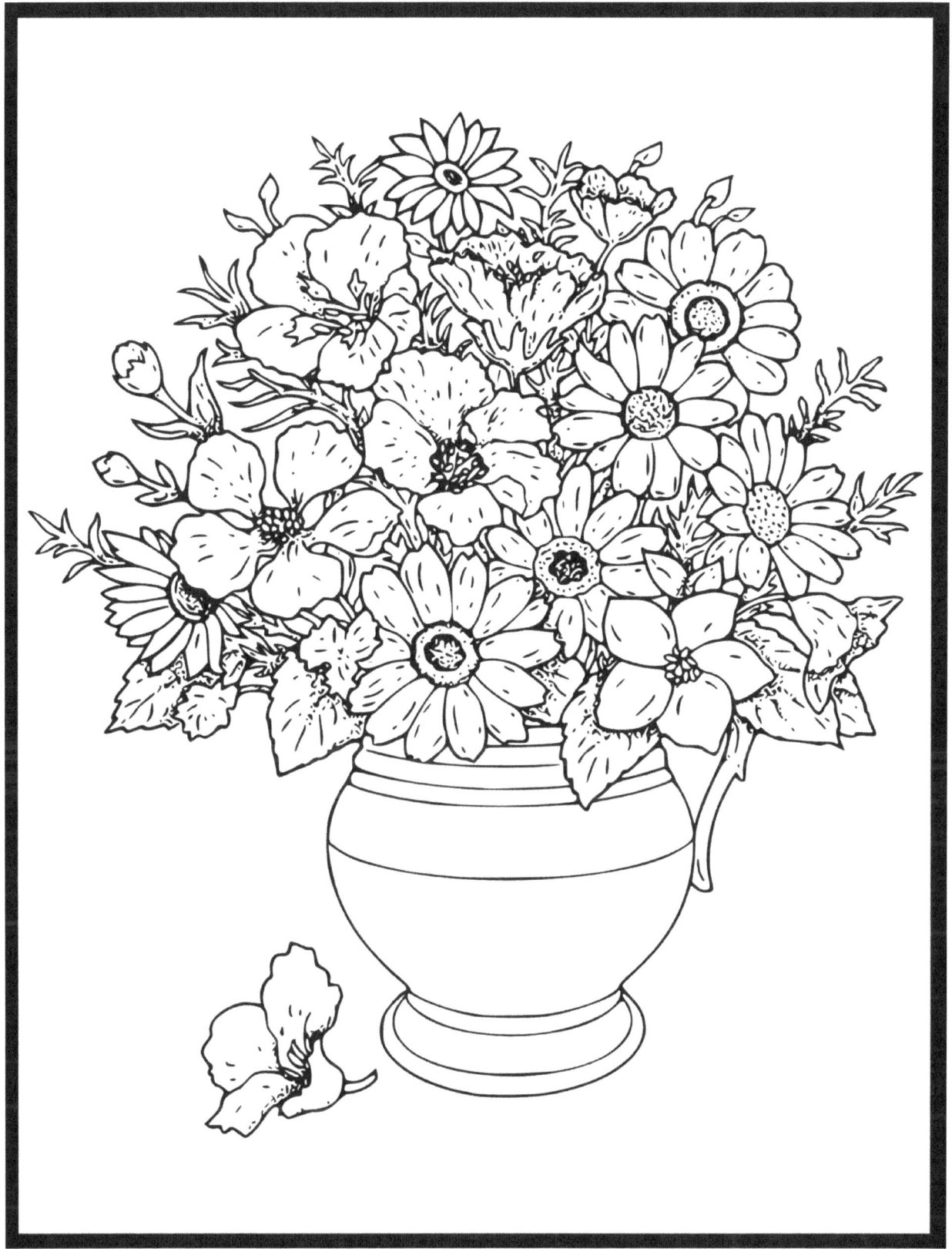

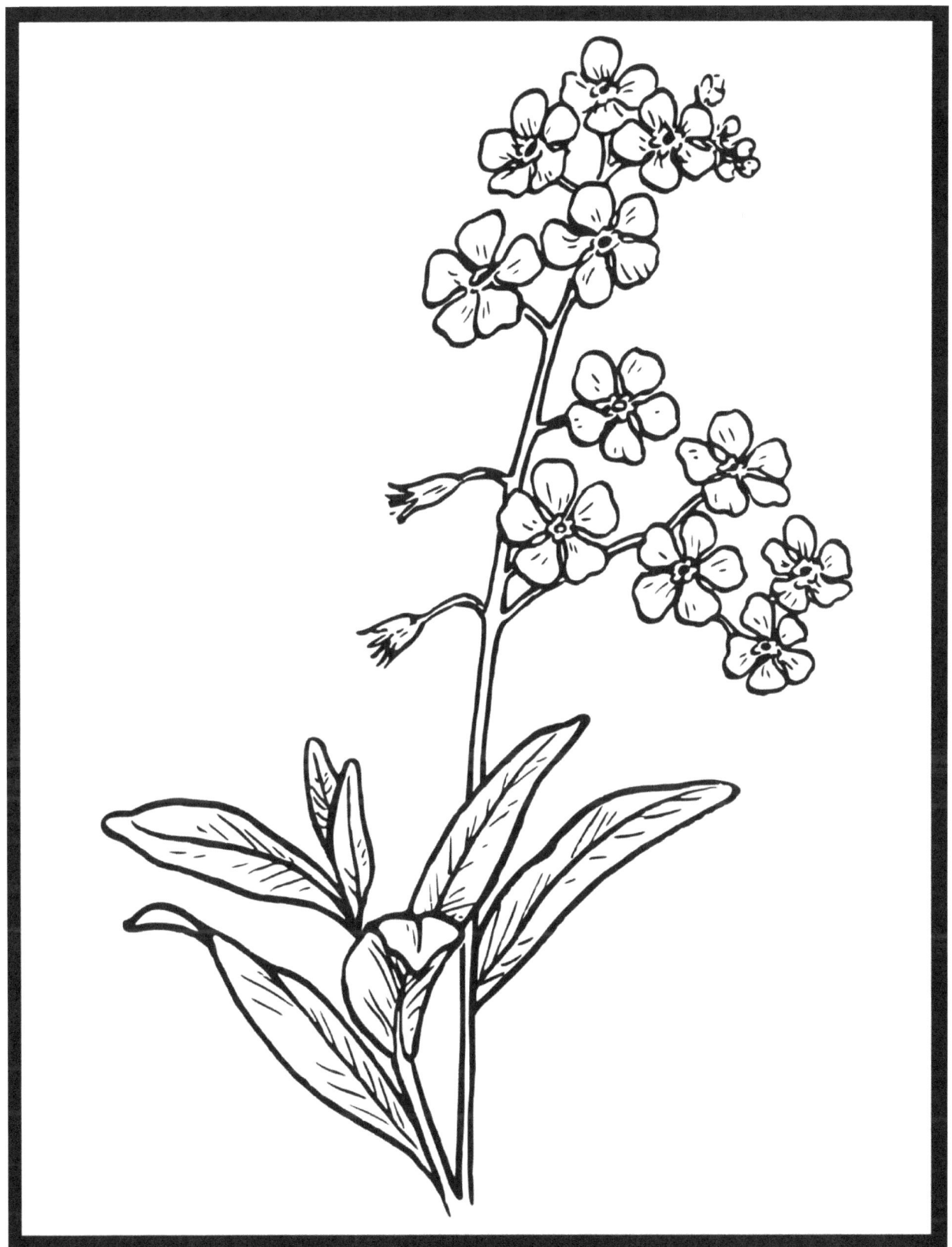

Floral Fantasies

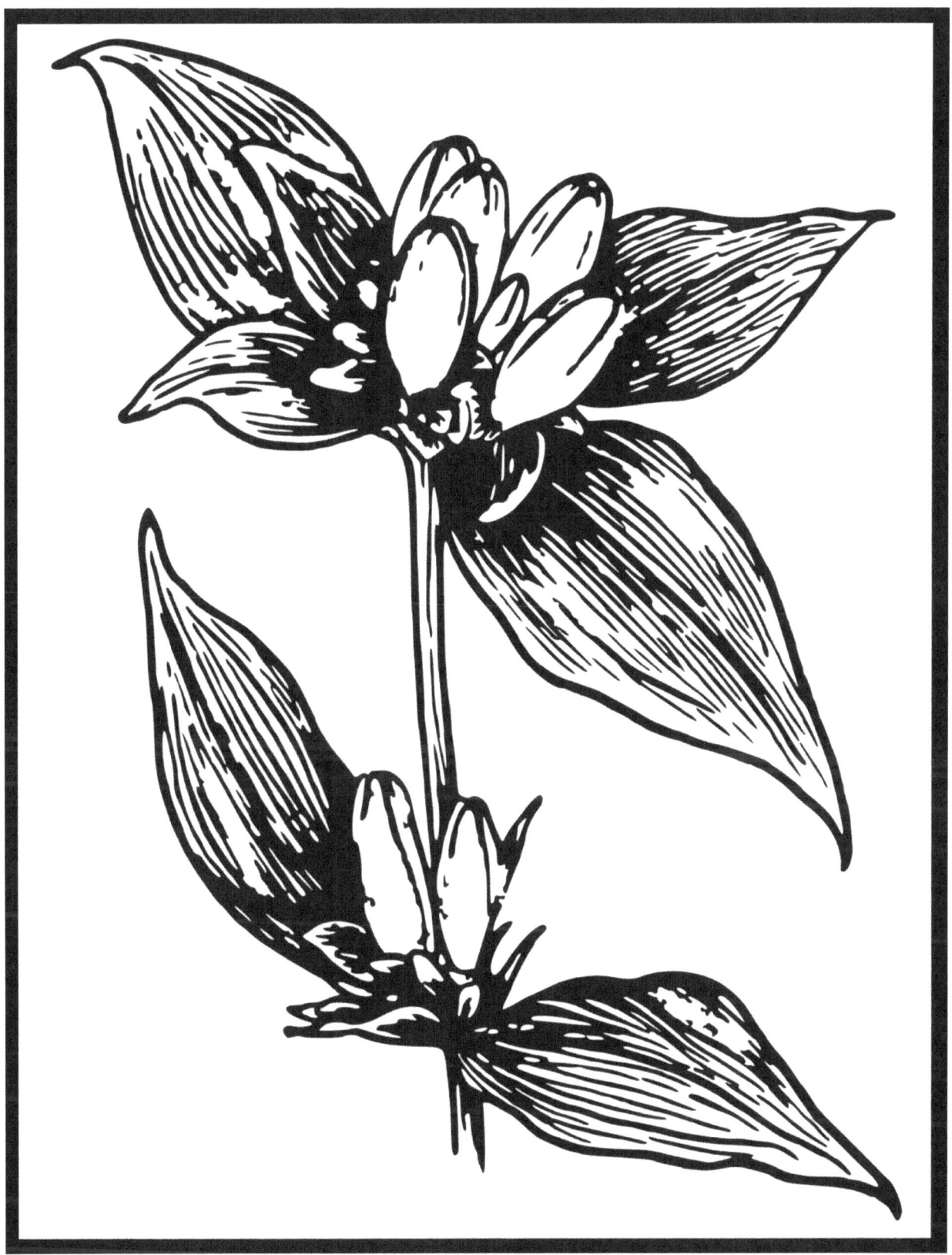

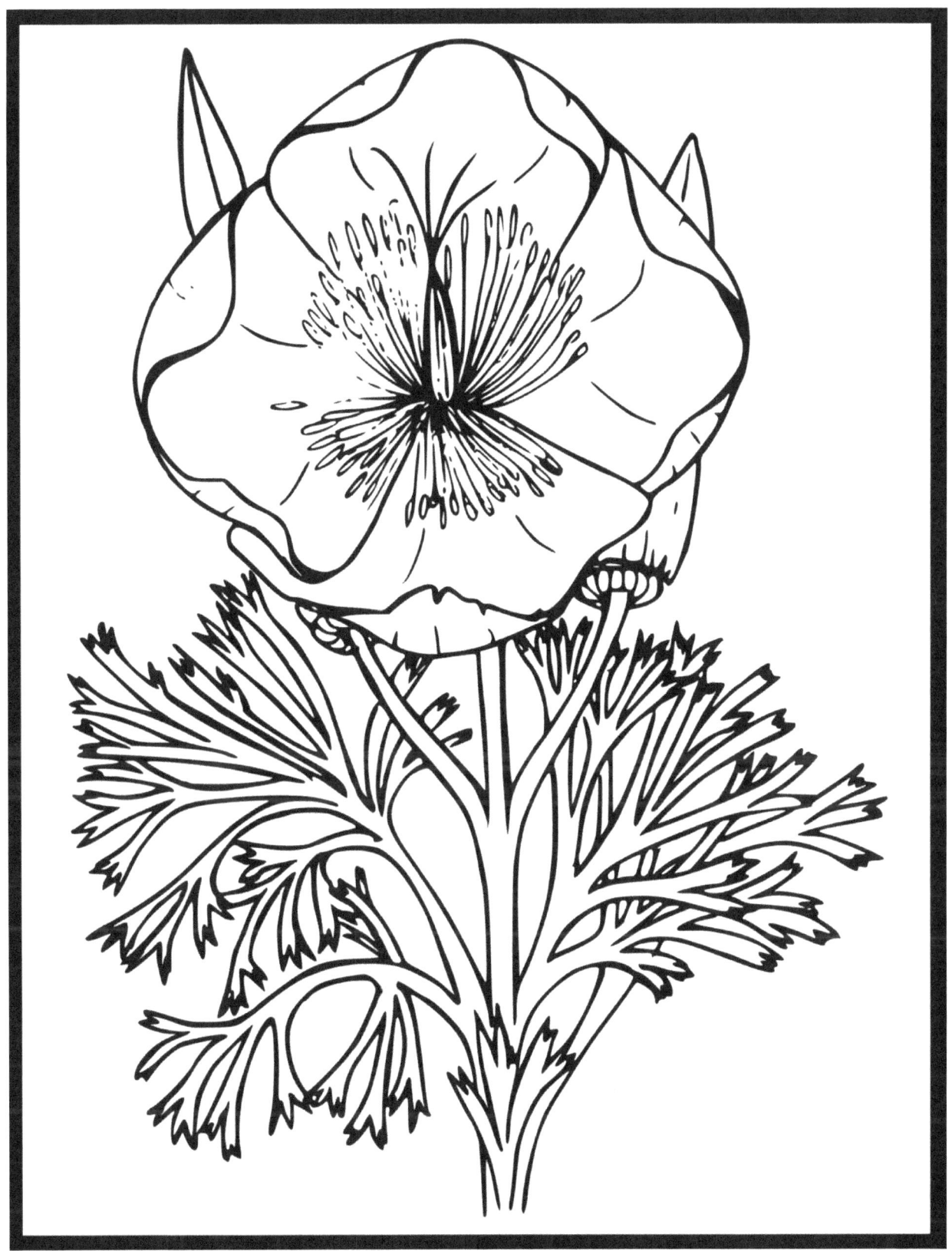

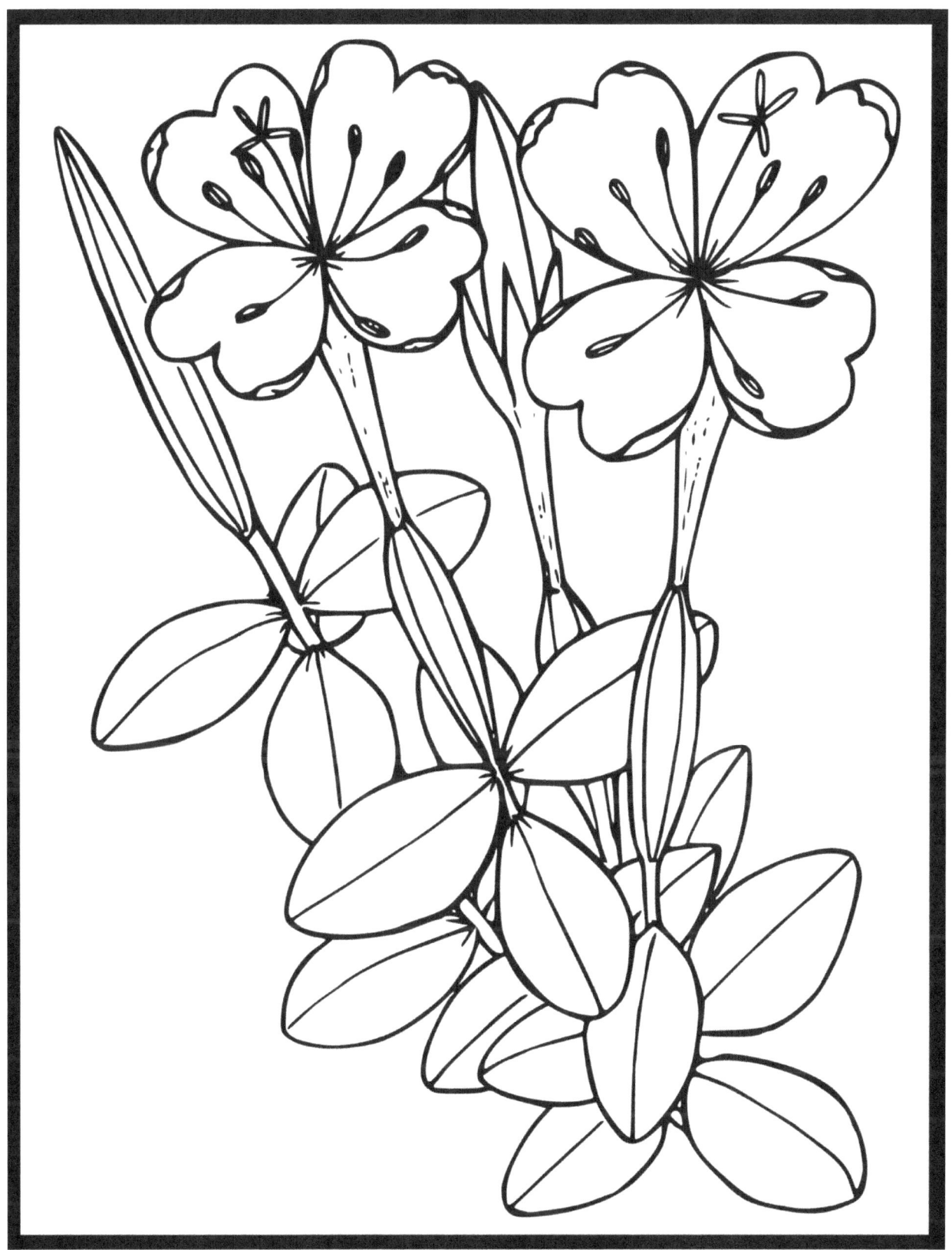

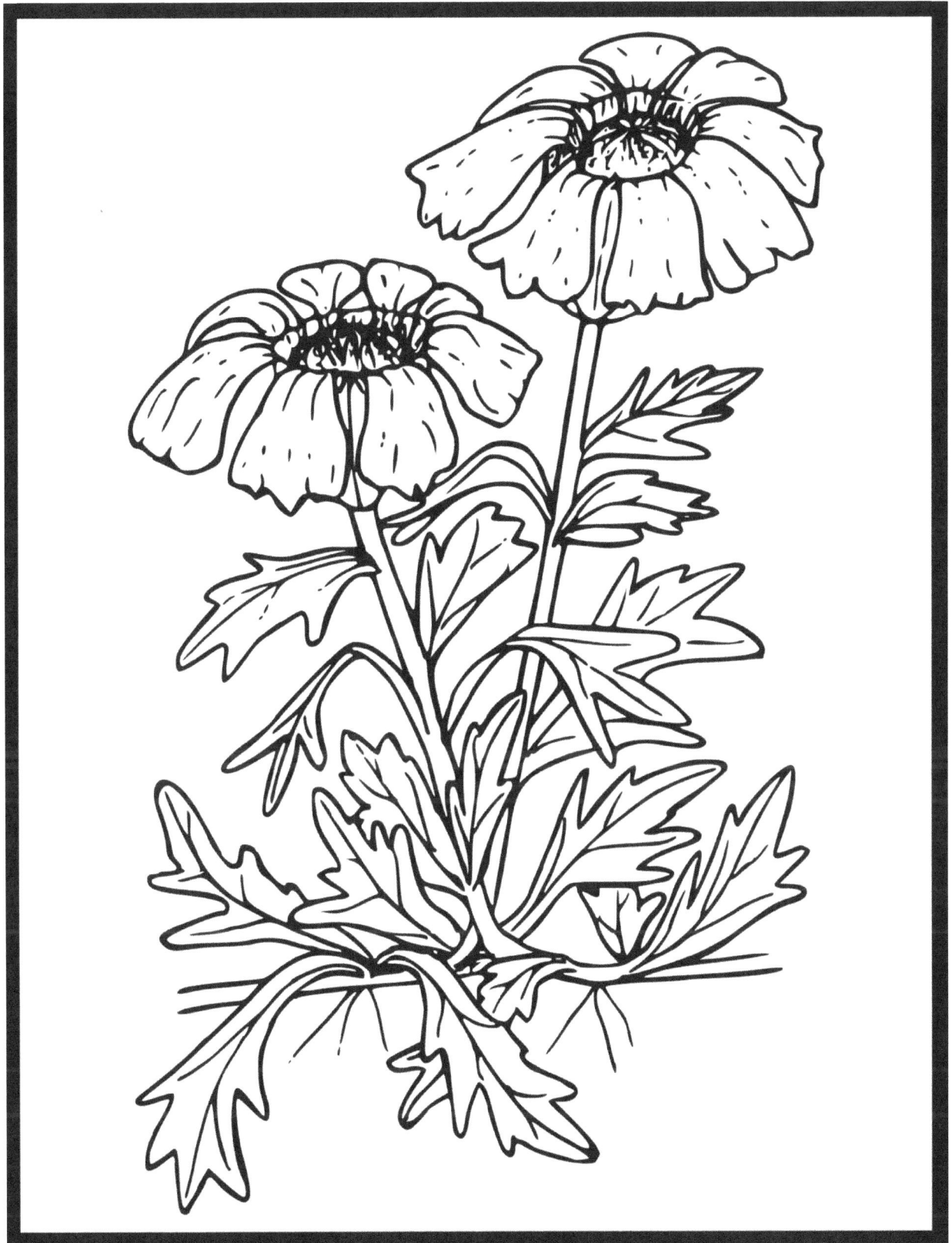

Floral Fantasies

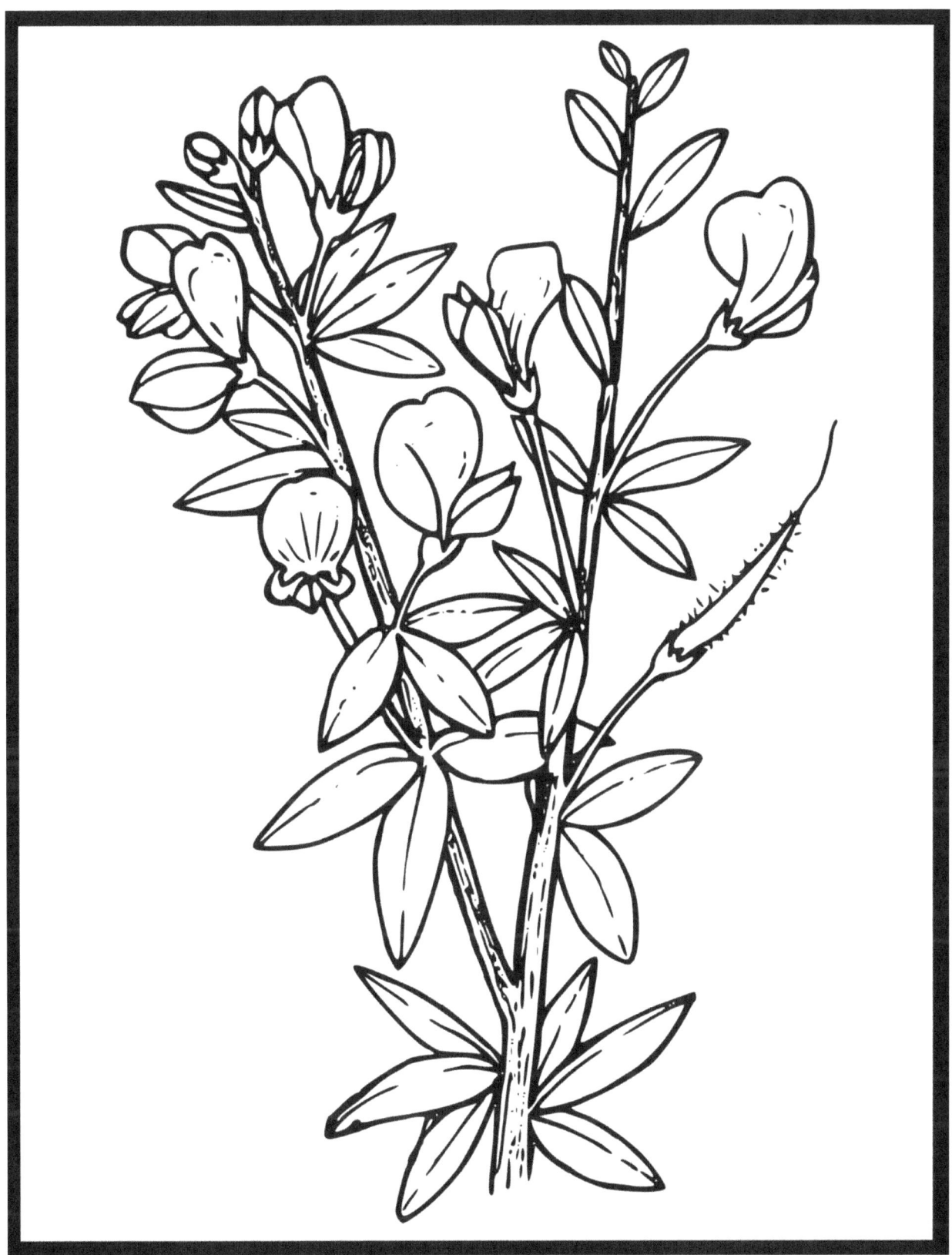

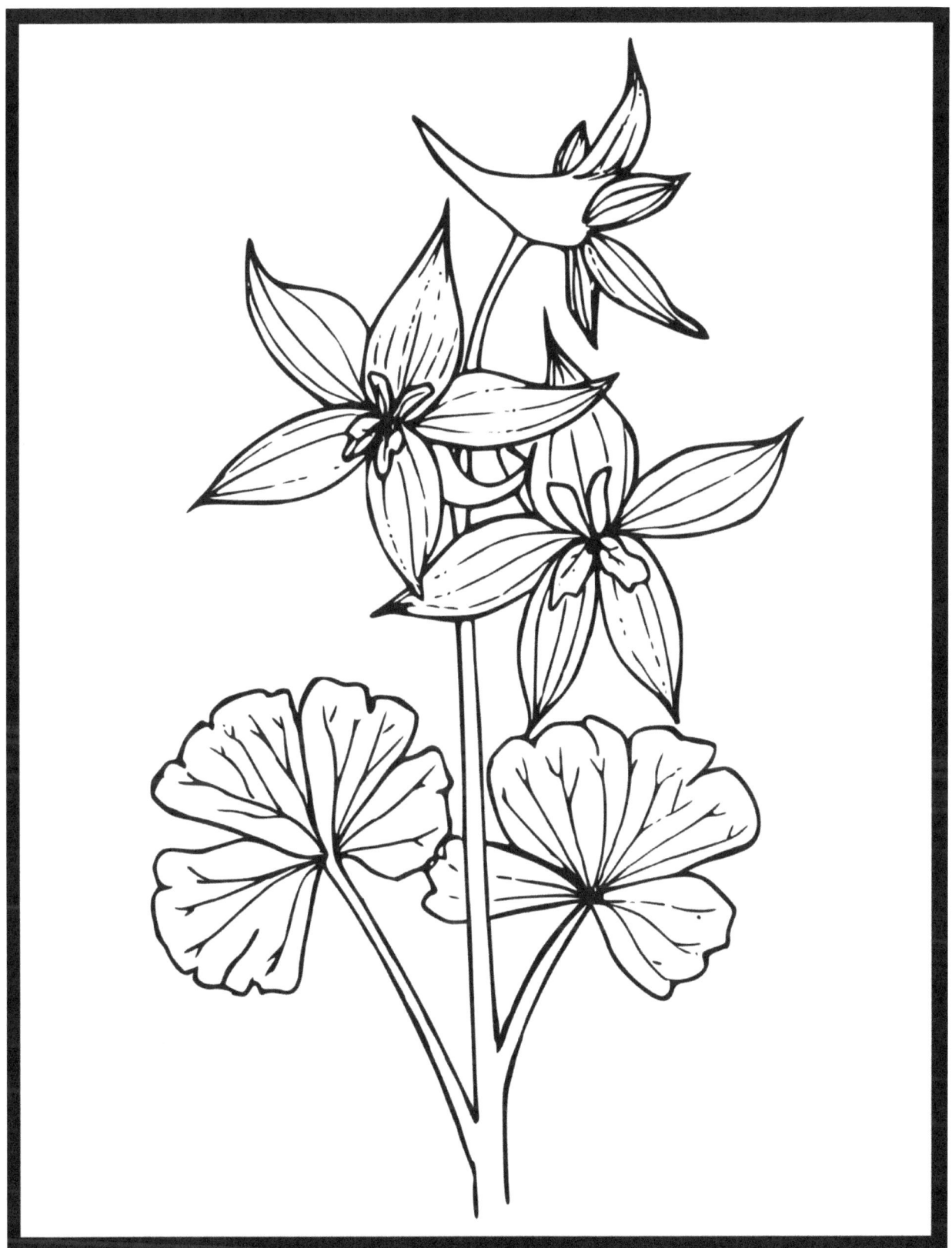

Floral Fantasies

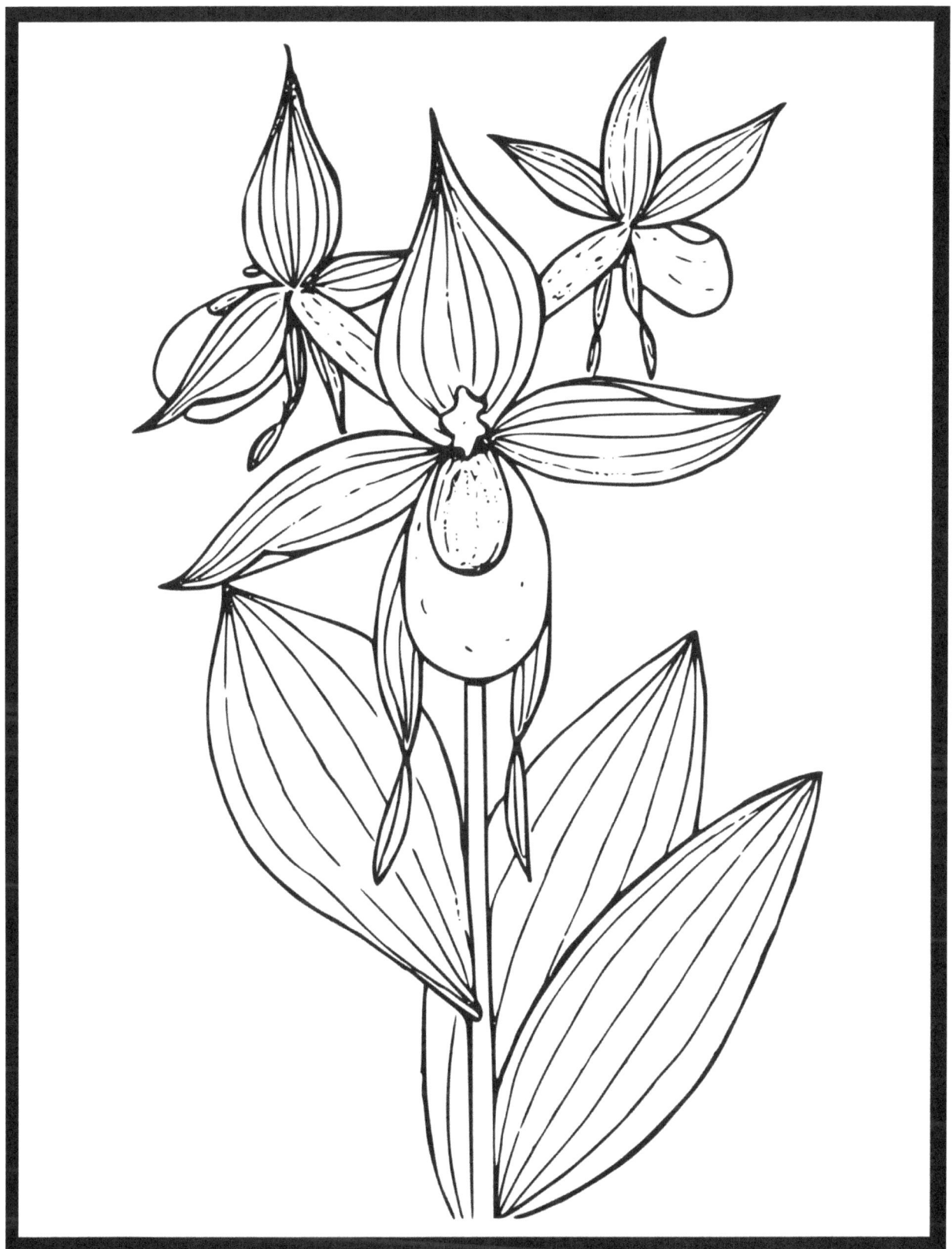

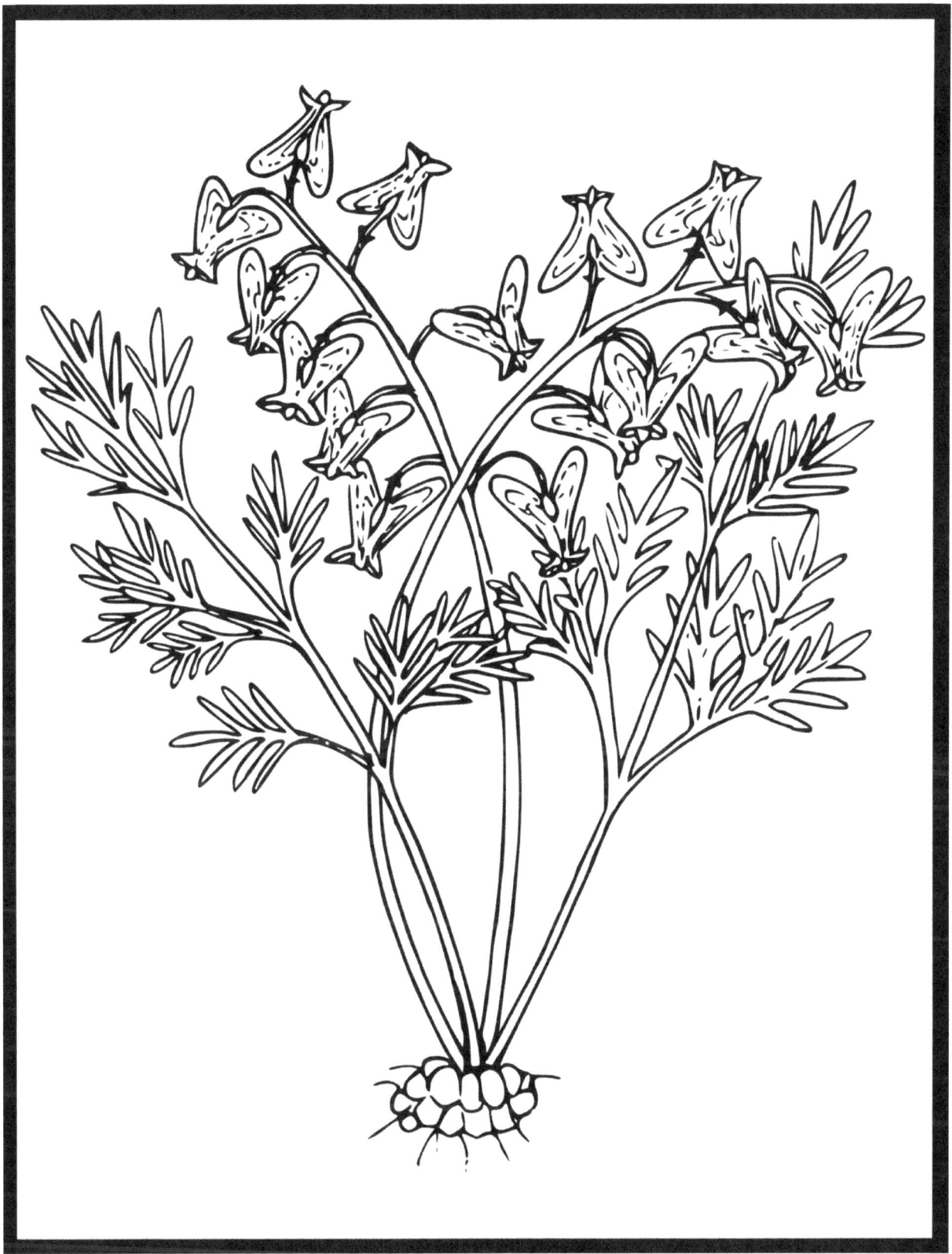

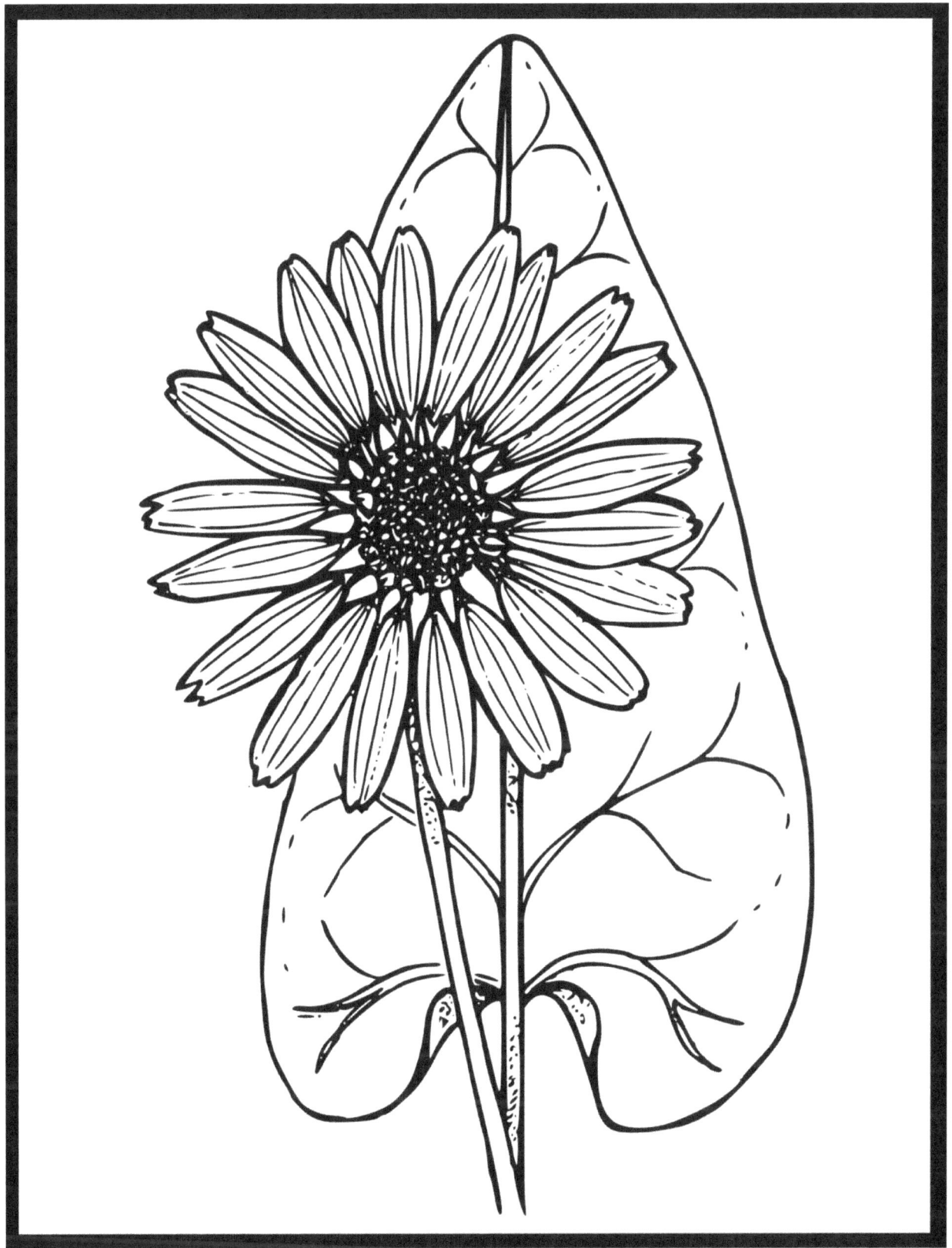

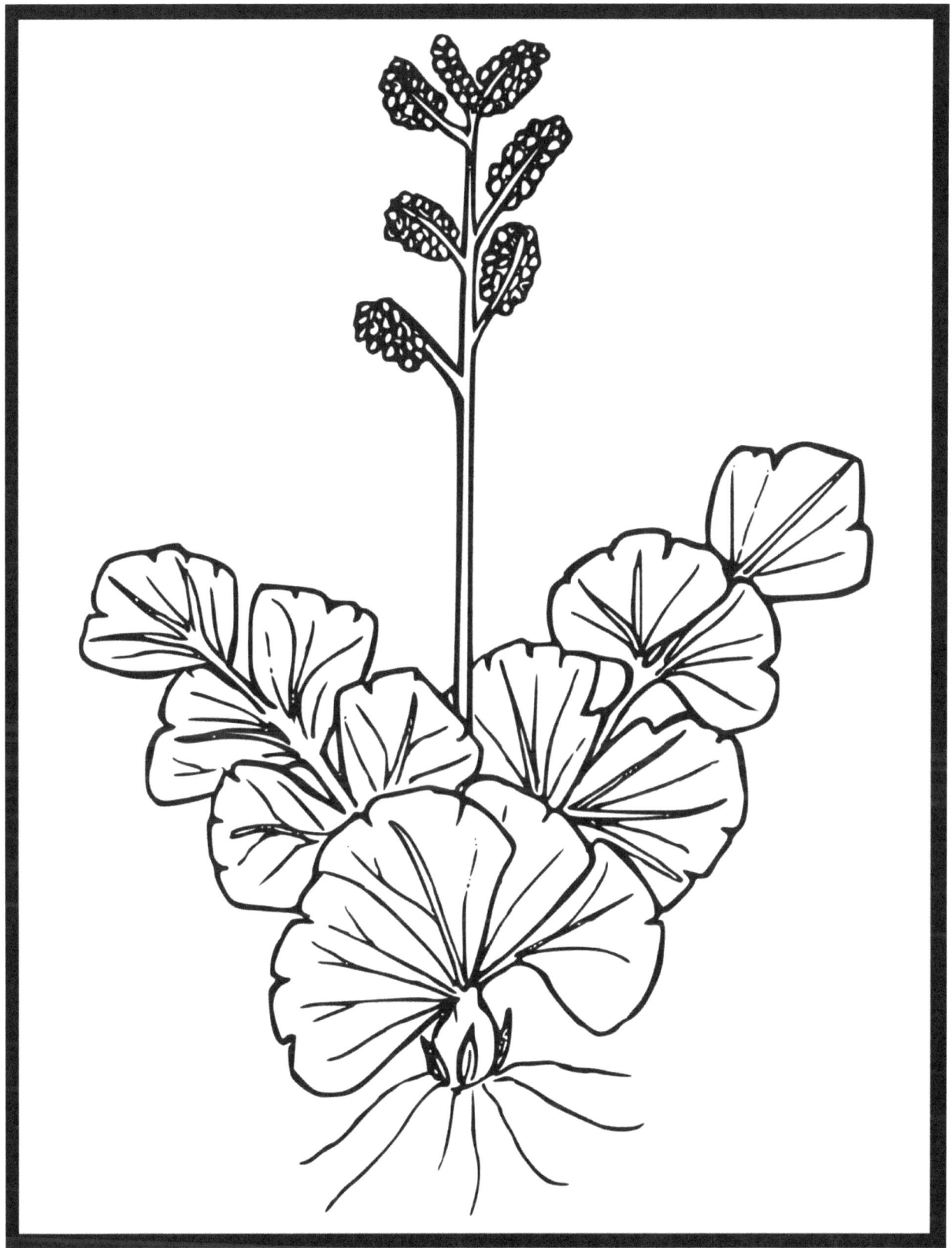

Floral Fantasies

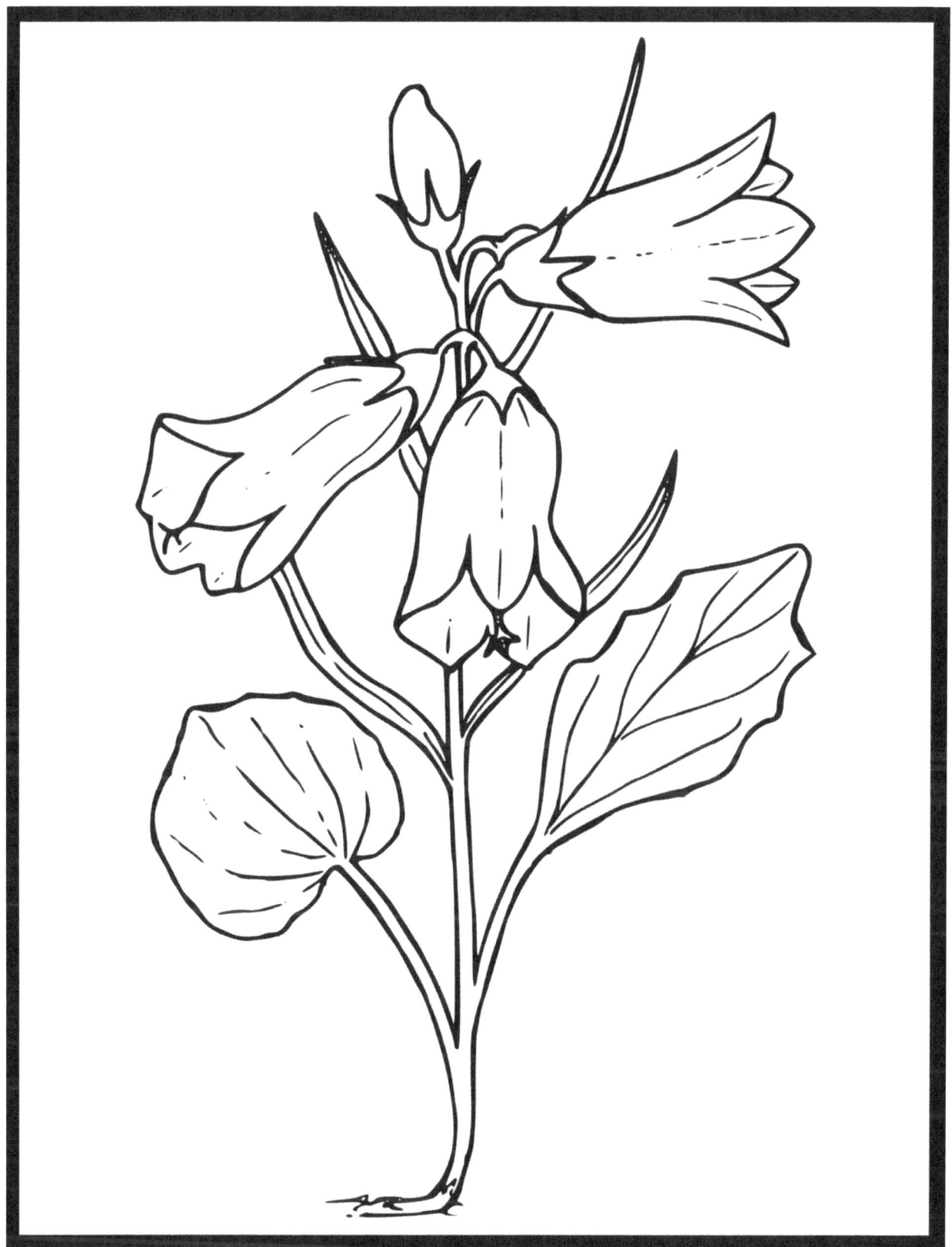

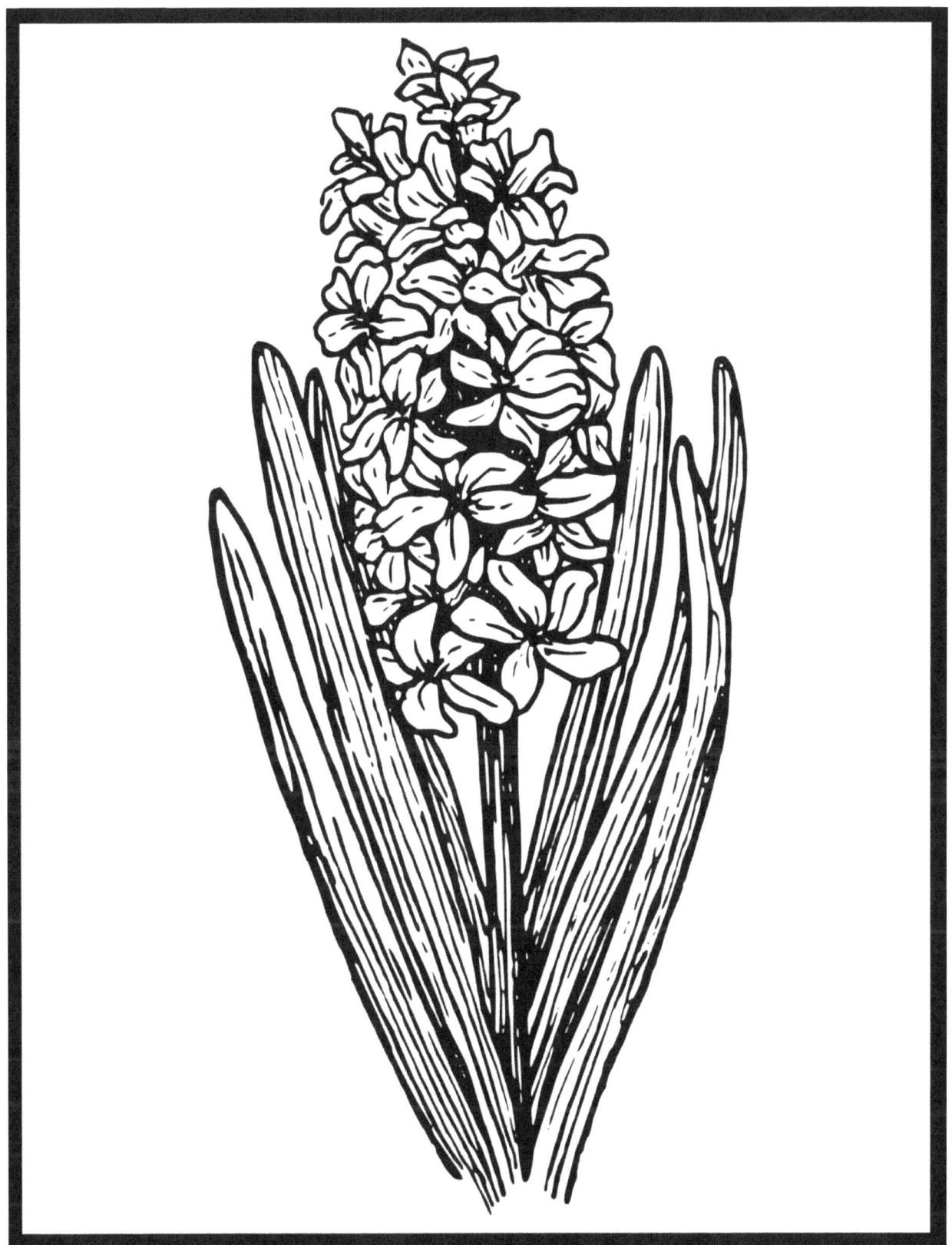

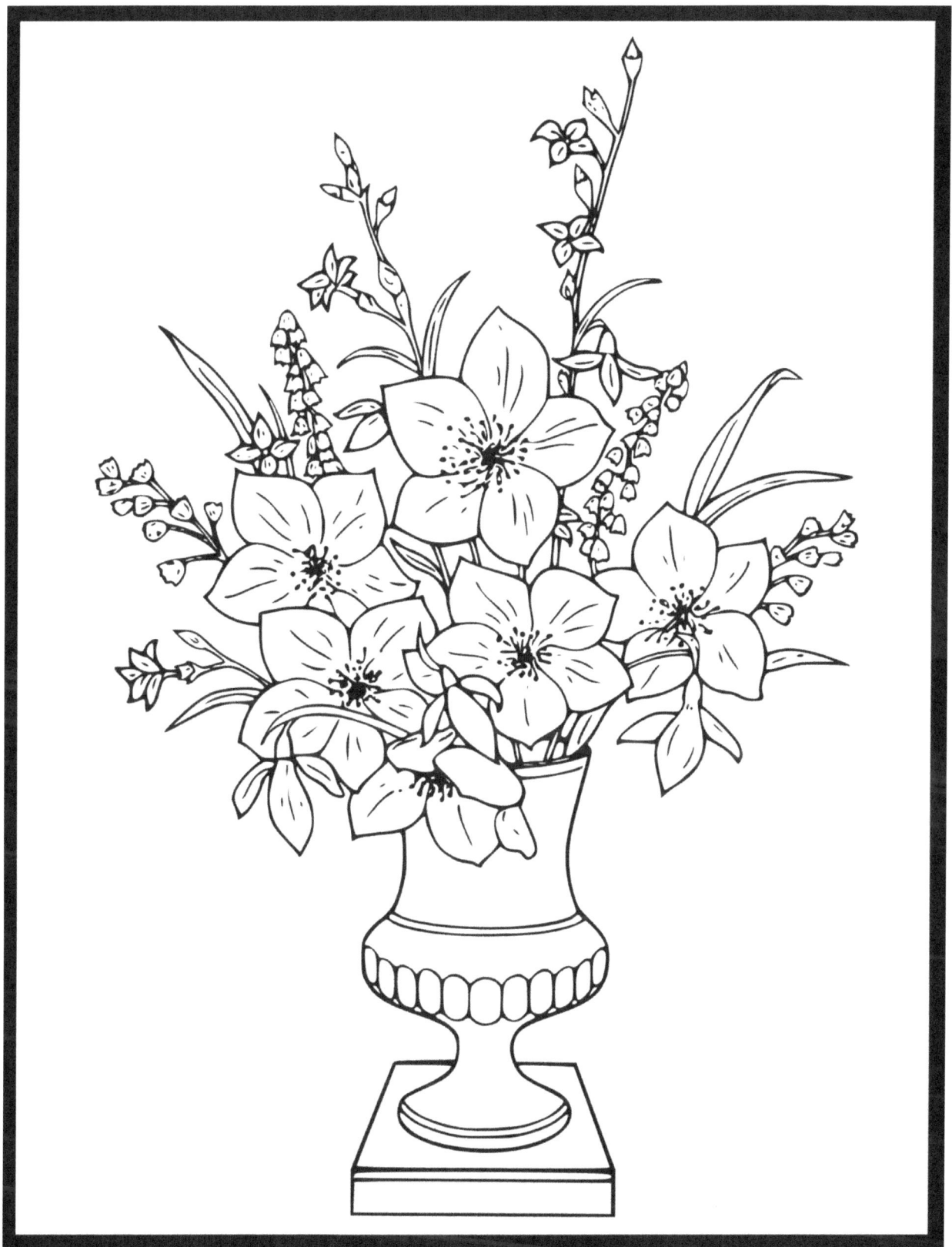

Floral Fantasies

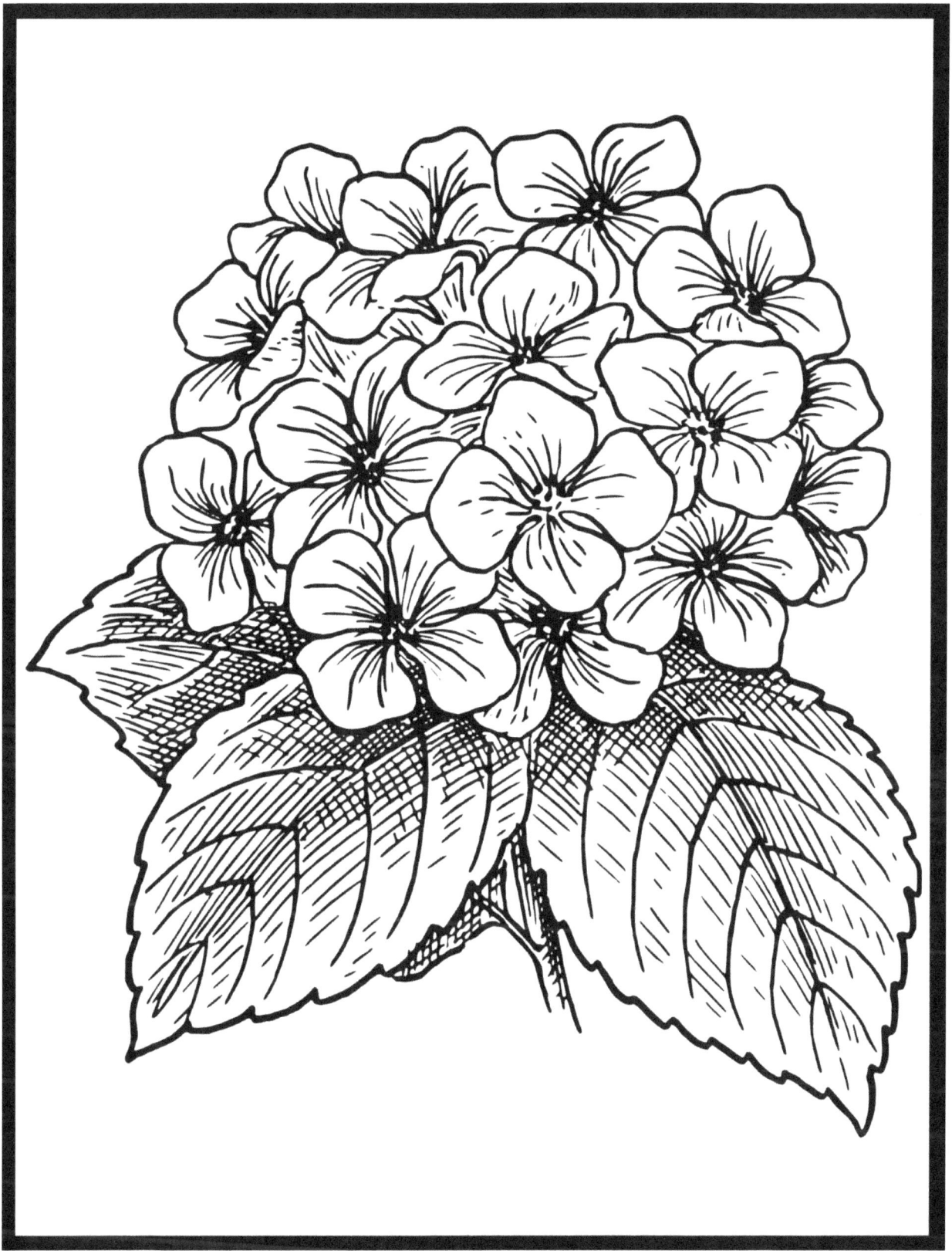

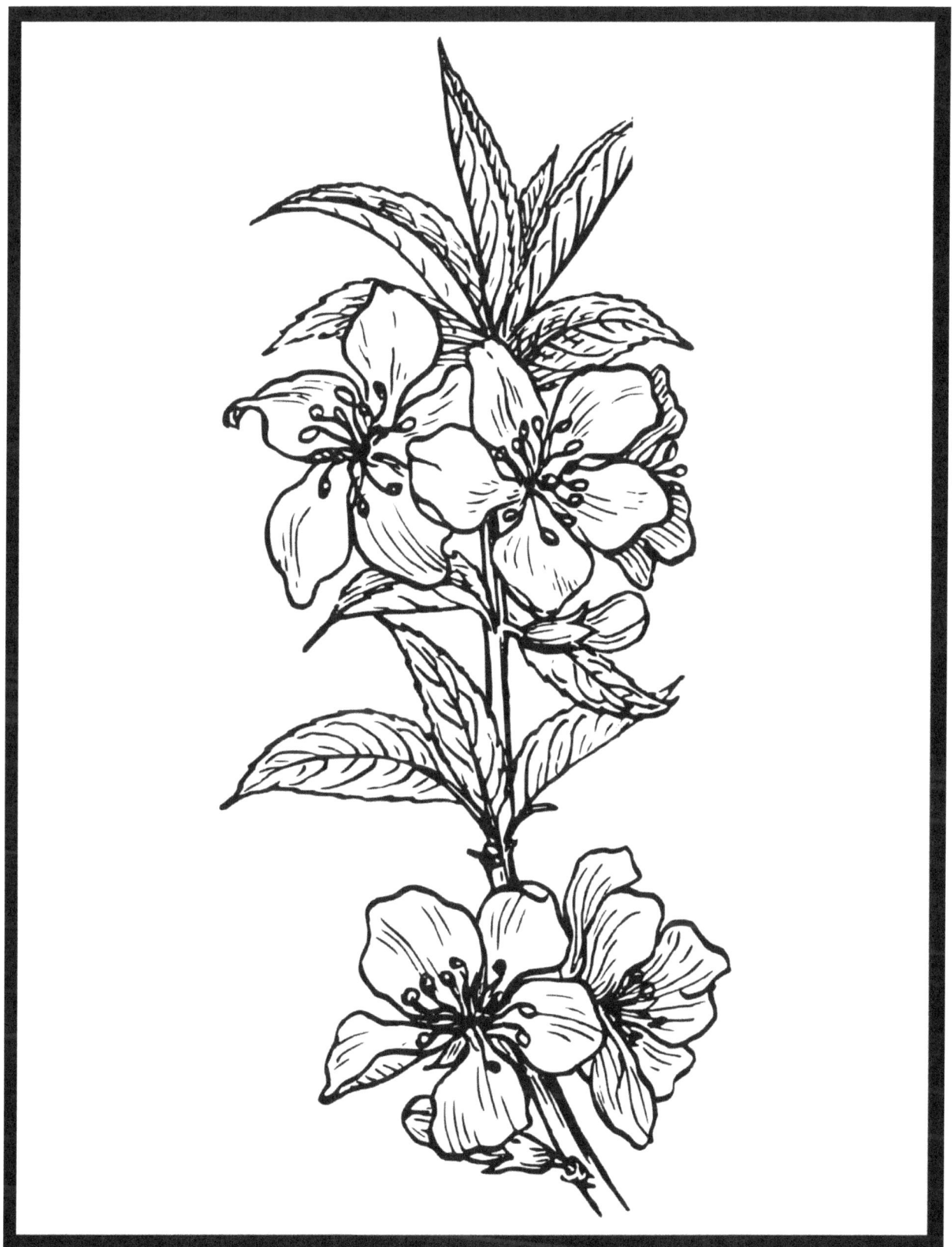

Floral Fantasies

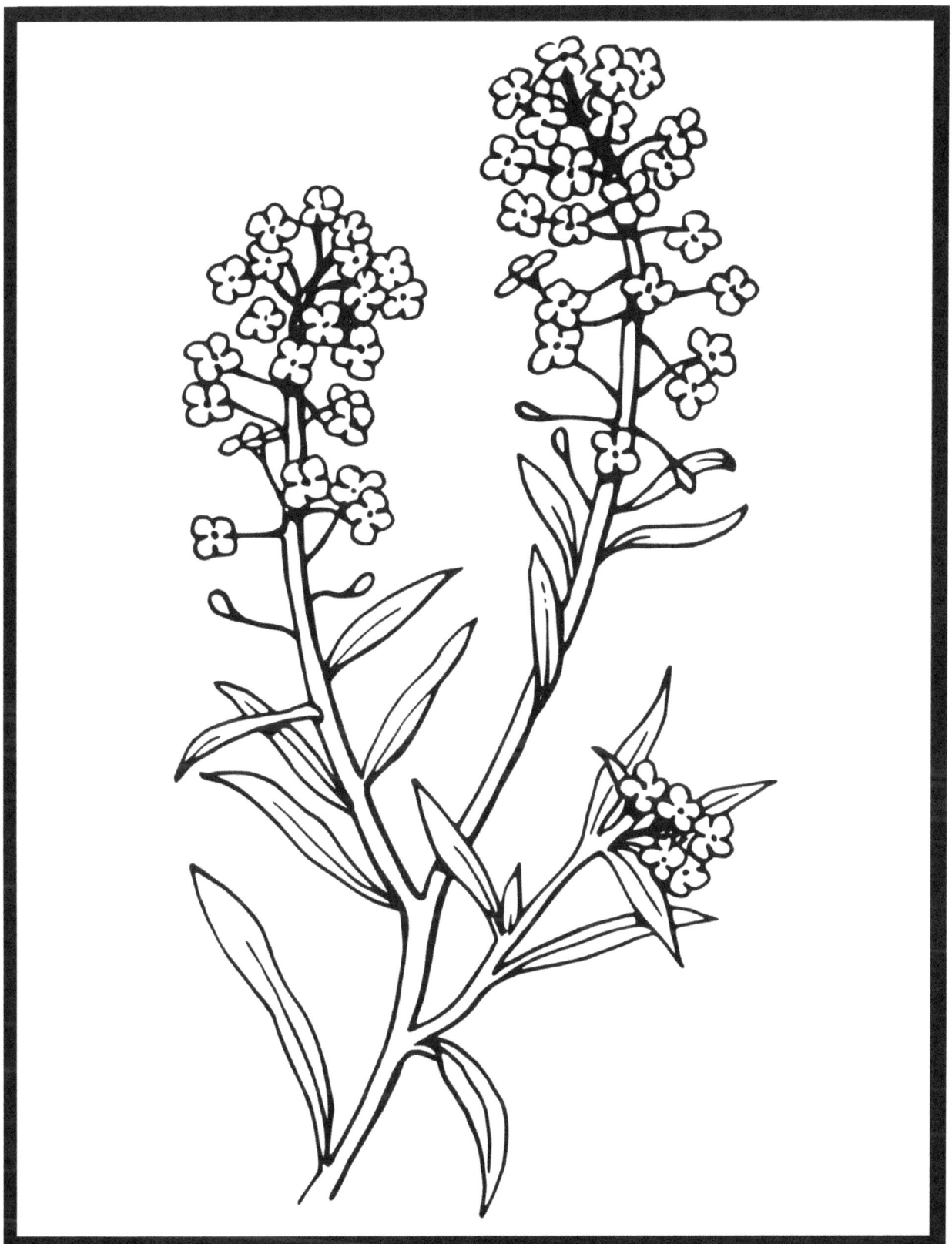

Floral Fantasies

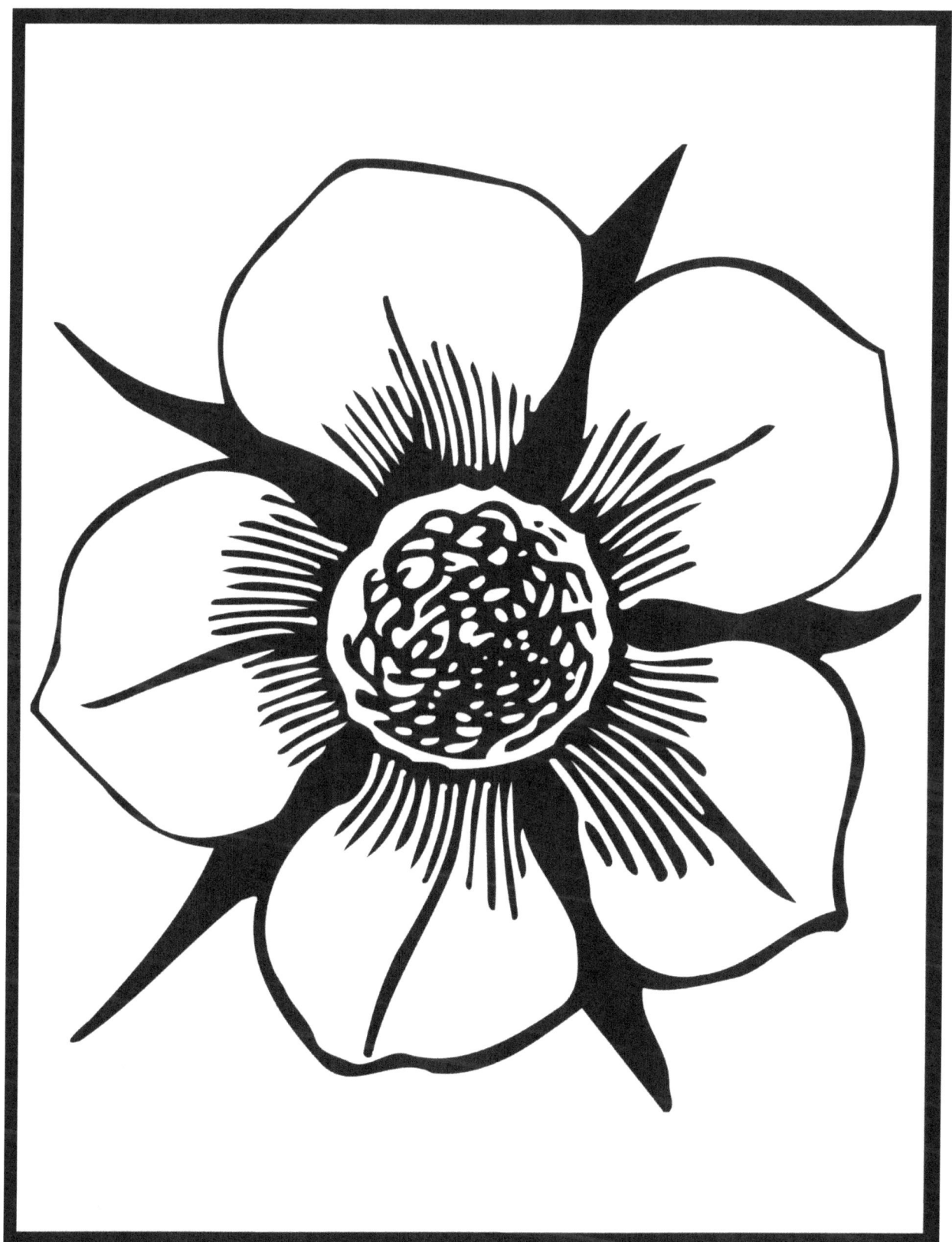

Floral Fantasies

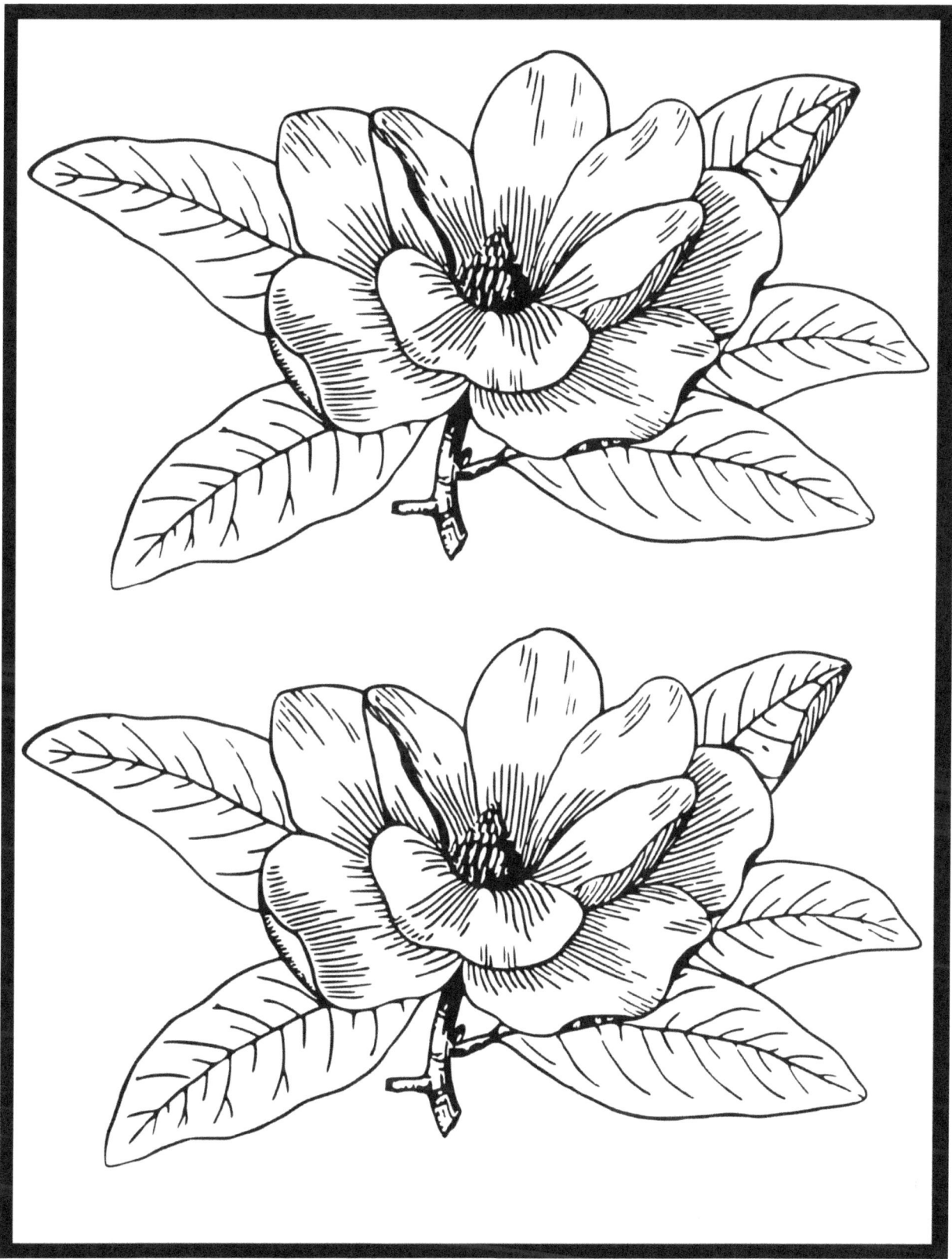

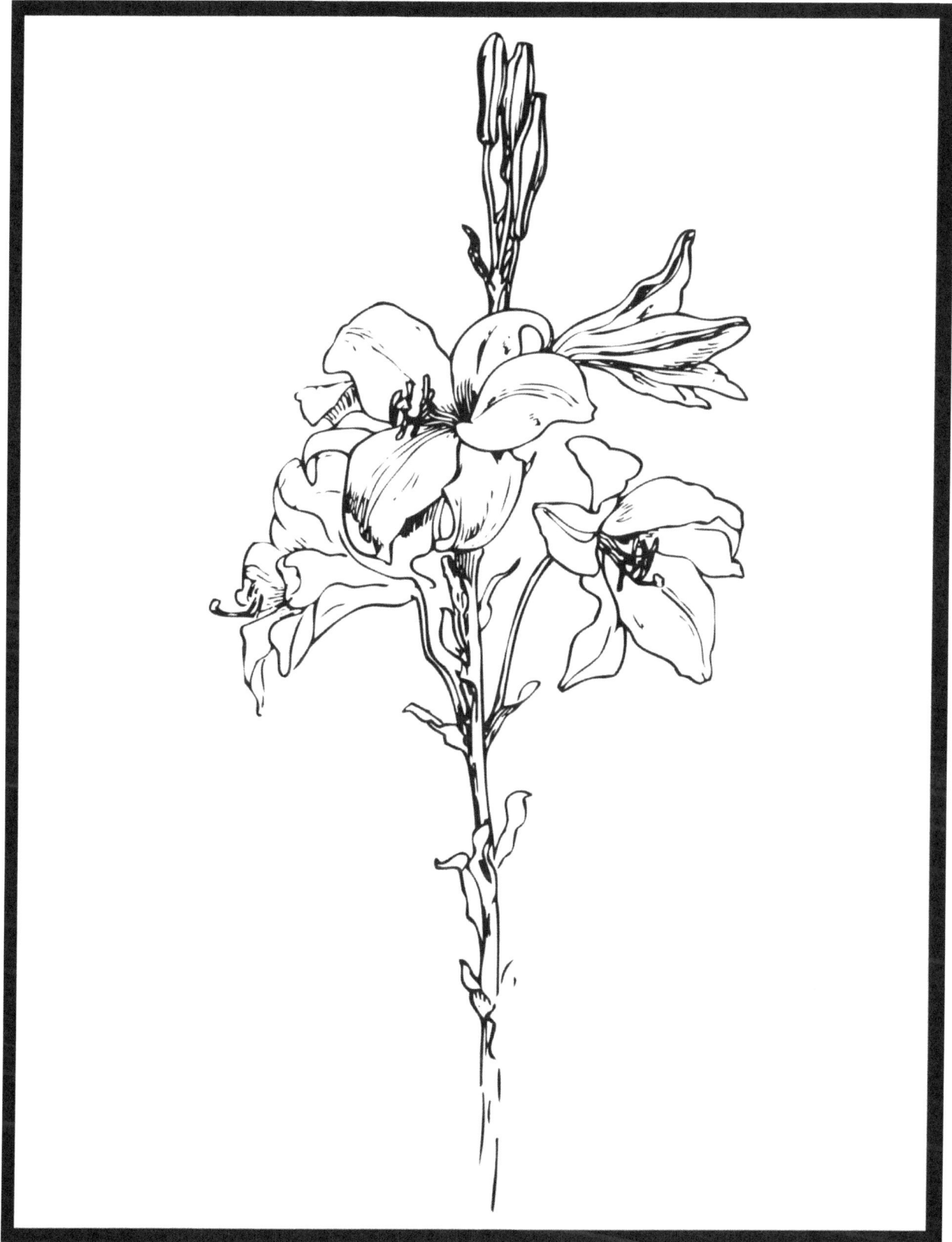

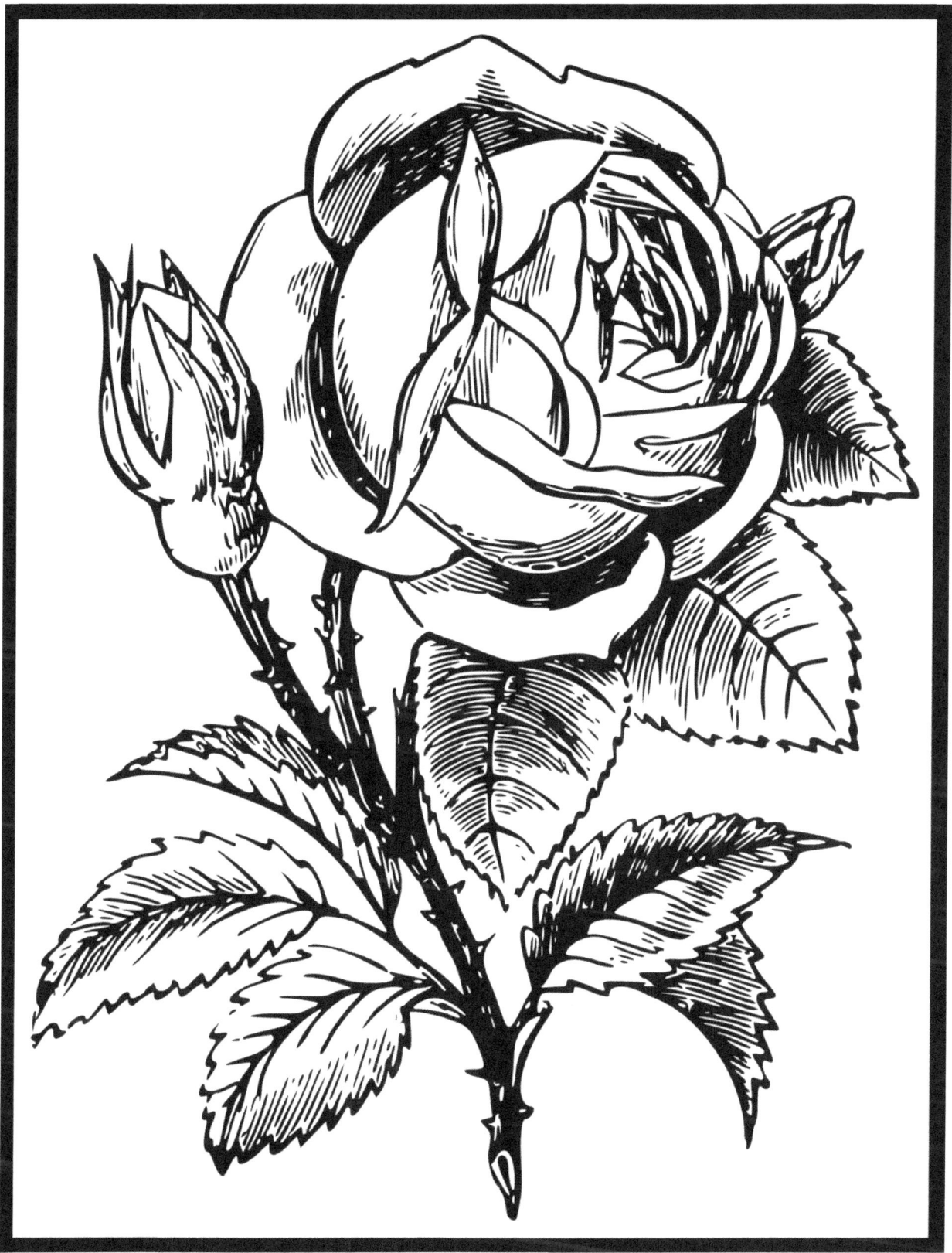

Floral Fantasies

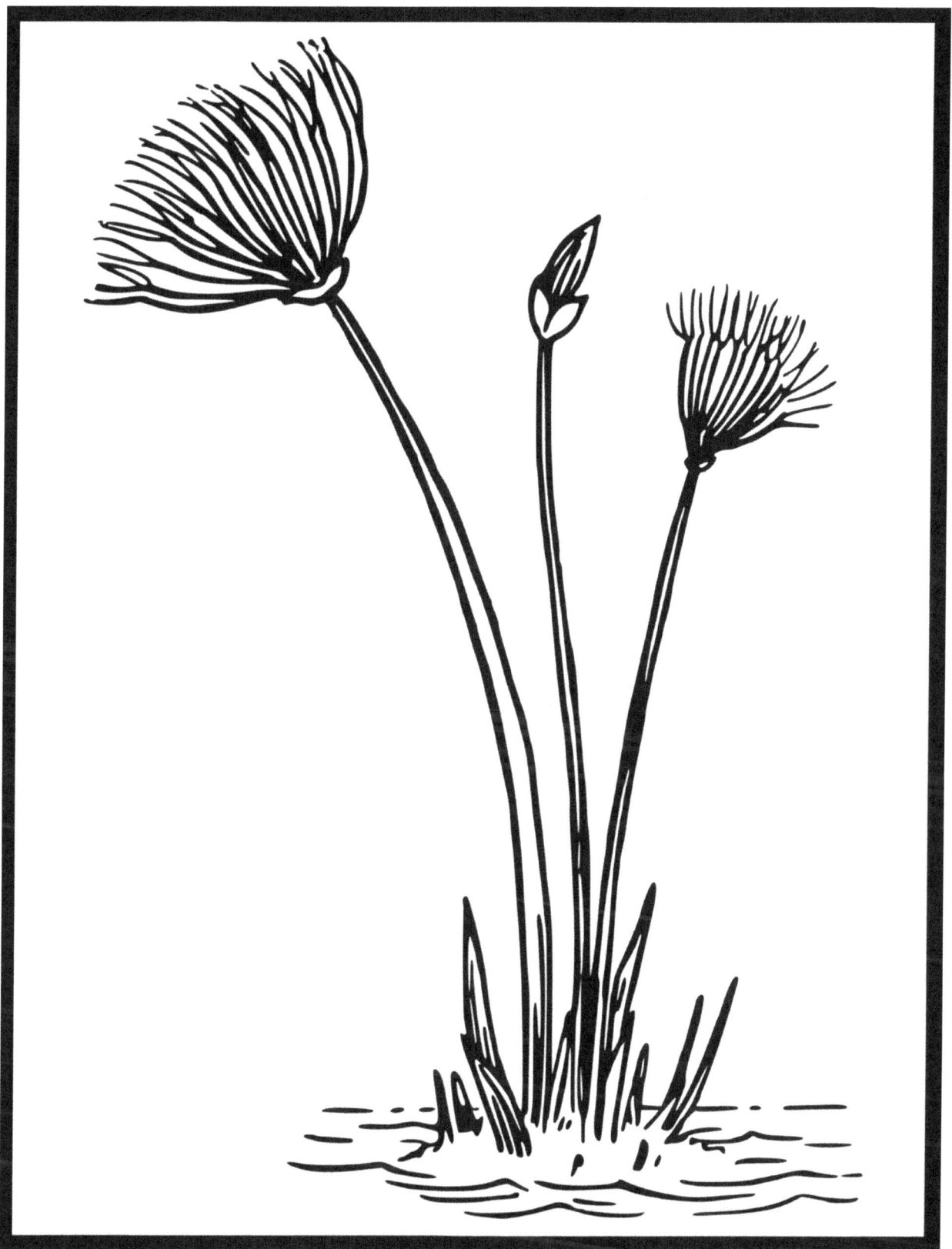

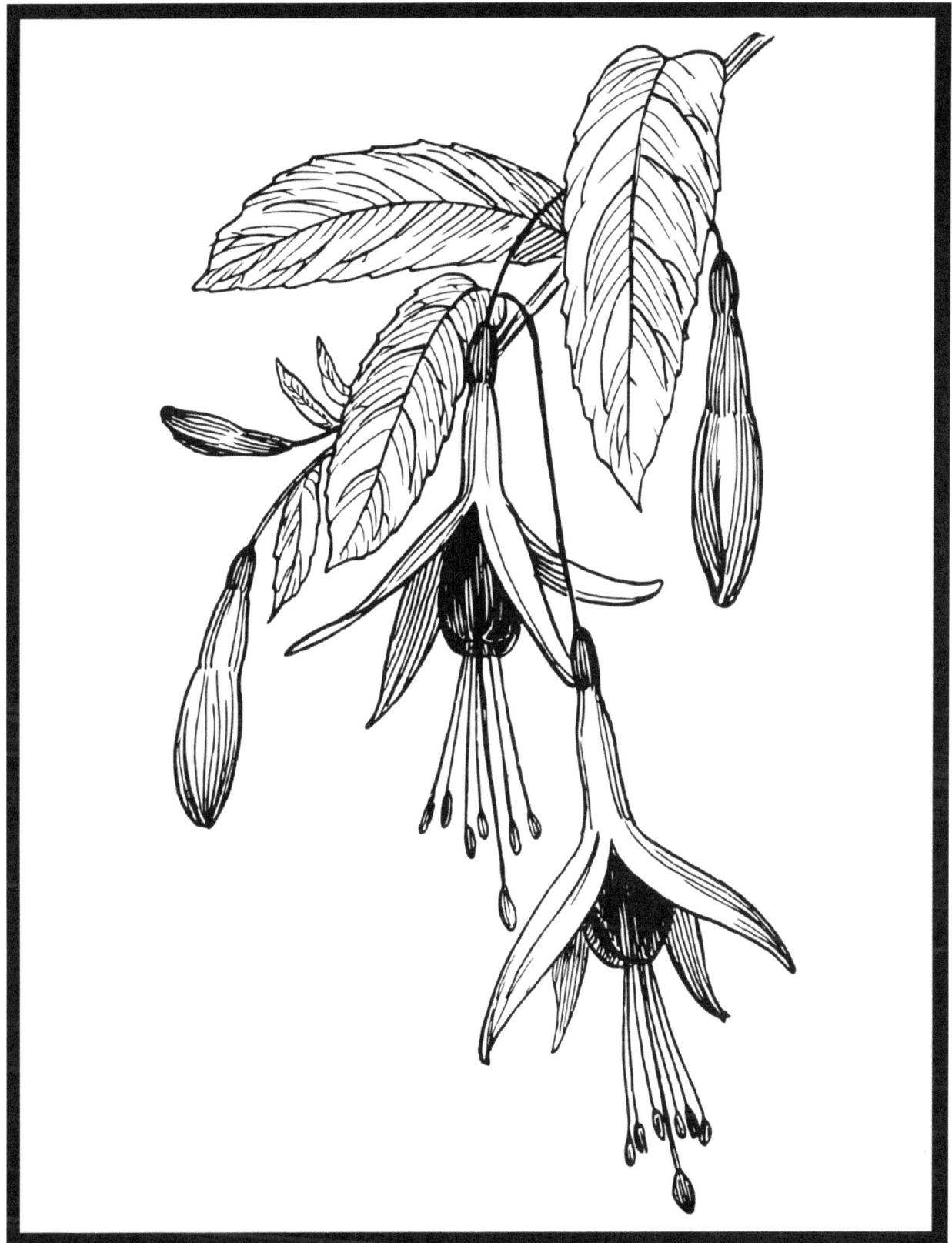

Floral Fantasies

ABOUT K. H. BURKETT

K. H. Burkett is a writer and artist from Southwest Virginia. She uses art to help her cope with the numerous mental health disorders she has. While she has no formal training in writing or art she has spent many years teaching herself different techniques. Throughout her journey as an artist her style and techniques have matured and while she still has a long road ahead of her in both artist and emotional growth she tries daily to better herself. The goal of her books is to help others explore their emotions and innermost thoughts by using art. She hopes to help others the way she was helps years ago.